BRITAIN AT WAR 1914~1919

Craig Mair

Principal Teacher of History,
Wallace High School, Stirling

John Murray

Also by Craig Mair

A Time in Turkey
A Star for Seamen
The Lighthouse Boy

© 1982 Craig Mair

First published 1982
by John Murray (Publishers) Ltd, 50 Albemarle Street,
London, W1X 4BD

Reprinted 1983, 1985, 1987, 1988, 1990, 1992, 1994, 1995

Printed and bound in Great Britain
at The Bath Press, Avon

British Library Cataloguing in Publication Data

Mair, Craig
   Britain at war 1914-1919
   1. World War, 1914-1918   2. Great Britain—
   History—George V, 1910-1936
   I. Title
   941.083   DA577

ISBN 0 7195 3877 7

Contents

Acknowledgements

I would like to thank friends, pupils, colleagues, particularly in the History Department at Falkirk High School, and numerous librarians, for their help, advice and constructive criticism while I tackled this work. Thanks are also due to Sandy Cowan for taking the photographs on pages 38 and 102, and to my wife Anne for valuable help with the text. Special thanks go to Evelyn Fairley and Fiona Swinton for reading the chapters so carefully and for their great help with the maps, photographs and captions.

I am also grateful to the following for permission to reproduce material from the sources indicated.

Printed material: B. T. Batsford, *The Battle of Jutland* by Geoffrey Bennett; Victor Gollancz, *War is War* by Ex-Private X; HMSO, *With a Machine Gun to Cambrai* by George Coppard; Hutchinson Publishing, *My War Memoirs* by General Ludendorff; Phoebus Publishing Company, *The History of the 20th Century*, copyright BPC Publishing, 1968; Skeffington Publishers, *Kiel and Jutland* by Commander G. von Hase; The Society of Authors, for the Estate of John Masefield, *Gallipoli*; Virtue & Co., *The Great War in Europe* by Frank R. Cana; also HEB, *A Military Atlas of the First World War* by Arthur Banks, and Weidenfeld & Nicolson, *First World War Atlas* by Martin Gilbert, from which many facts and figures were obtained.

Illustrations: Falkirk District Museum, p.98; *Illustrated London News* Picture Library, 83; Imperial War Museum, front and back covers, 12, 16, 27, 28, 31, 32, 33, 34, 36, 39, 41, 42, 43, 44, 45, 47, 49, 51, 53, 55, 56, 58, 59, 60, 61, 68, 69, 70, 71, 72, 74, 77, 78, 82, 85, 87, 89, 90, 91, 92, 94, 96, 99, 100, 101, 108, 111, 112, 118, 119; Mrs M. MacGregor, 38; Mansell Collection, 18; Mrs J. Mason, 102; *Punch* Picture Library, 26; Radio Times Hulton Picture Library, 3, 4, 5, 7, 8, 25, 65, 93, 104, 106, 107.

Author's Note

Although the shooting stopped in November 1918 World War One did not officially end until the peace treaty was signed in mid-1919, and many war memorials all over Britain bear the dates 1914-1919.

1 Britain before the War

In 1900 Britain was the greatest nation on earth. Queen Victoria, now an old lady, had been ruling since 1837 and during her reign Britain and her colonies had grown into the largest and most powerful empire ever seen. Britain ruled about one quarter of the world, including the 'dominions' of Canada, Australia and New Zealand, plus many colonies in Africa, Asia, the West Indies, India and the Pacific Islands. These lands were so extensive that it was said 'the sun never sets on the British Empire'.

Britain was also very powerful. The Royal Navy, twice the size of any other fleet, controlled the sea, protecting the merchant ships which brought goods from the empire to Britain. Meanwhile at home, industries like textiles, iron, coal, engineering and shipbuilding made Britain a strong business and trading nation too.

Queen Victoria died in 1901 and was followed by her son, King Edward VII. He died in 1910 and was succeeded by his son, King George V. Nevertheless, the whole period from 1900 to 1914, when the First World War began, is usually known as the Edwardian era—a time when Britain seemed to be at the very peak of industrial power, empire building and great achievement.

The two main political parties at this time were the Liberals and the Conservatives. In the 1906 general election the Liberals and their supporters won a large majority of about 250 seats in the House of Commons. This huge victory was soon nicknamed the 'Liberal Landslide' and the Scottish leader of the Liberals, Sir Henry Campbell-Bannerman, became Prime Minister. He died in 1908 and was replaced by Mr Herbert Asquith, who was still Prime Minister when war began.

Although the Edwardian era was one of British imperial power and industrial strength, it also meant poverty and hardship for many people. While Britain's industries made the country strong and some people very rich, this wealth remained in the hands of only a few. The workers who toiled daily in dreadful mills and factories, and who lived in slums, remained poor. The Liberals tried to tackle this problem of poverty (see page 3), but some historians have said that even in 1914 Britain was still inhabited by two nations—the rich and the poor.

Rich and poor

In 1900 people in Britain were divided into three general groups, mostly depending on how much money they earned. These were the lower, or working, class; the middle class; and the upper class. Today the differences between these groups are not so clear, but during the Edwardian period the divisions were much sharper. Although it was possible to move up in life, by luck or hard work, most people had little opportunity of changing to a different class.

Of the three classes, the upper class was easily the smallest group. It included people who on the whole did not have to work for a living—generally titled people or rich landowners who could live off the income from renting their land to farmers. Some people did work, usually in Parliament, the Church or the Army, or as the head of a large business, but they did not *need* to work. Members of Parliament, for example, were not paid before 1911.

Life for the rich was very enjoyable. They lived in large houses, often surrounded by beautiful estates and attended by many servants and workers. For cooks and maids the

1

work of baking or cleaning and scrubbing was constant, although some houses now had electric lighting and a few even had the recently invented vacuum cleaner. Some houses also had a telephone, though it looked nothing like the telephones of today.

For most rich people, life was centred on parties and social events such as fox-hunting or grouse-shooting, racing at Ascot or tennis at Wimbledon. Many went abroad for the winter to warmer weather or the winter sports. Many wealthy families also owned a motor car (it is estimated that there were about 130,000 cars in Britain in 1914), and a few very adventurous young men were even flying the recently invented aeroplane. Although many people were concerned with the lives of their servants or workers, life in upper-class society was all they really knew. They knew nothing of slum conditions or pawn shops. Ladies never even got their hands dirty. Indeed many had more in common with the rich from Europe or America than with the poor in Britain. Upper-class life was, in fact, a world of its own.

Middle-class people were generally not as rich as the upper-class landowners but many of them were nevertheless quite well off. They included businessmen, managers, and such professional people as doctors, lawyers, engineers, architects and accountants. Although they spent long hours at the factory or office, the work was not dirty or physically exhausting, and when it was over they could return to a pleasant life with a few servants in a large suburban house well away from the slum parts of the town. Some people even had a motor car, and most had at least a month's holiday, often spent by the sea in a fashionable holiday resort. Many were rich enough to rent a country cottage at weekends for fishing or shooting. They ate well and had few worries about unemployment or paying the doctor's bills. It was a far cry from the pleasures of upper-class life, but it was just as far from the problems of the working class.

Of Britain's population of 41 million, 80 per cent or about 35 million belonged to the working class. Within this class, however, there were wide differences. Skilled workers, who might earn £2 a week, were best off. They lived in small but comfortable terraced houses, usually with three or four rooms and perhaps a water pump in the kitchen. The family could eat quite well—meals might include soup, cheese, meat or fish. Sometimes there was even enough money left over to enable them to belong to a Friendly Society. In return for a regular weekly contribution the society would pay the doctor's bills if sickness struck the family.

Very few workers had paid holidays but some took a week's unpaid summer break, and everyone was entitled to Bank Holidays. Then they would escape to the seaside by cheap excursion train for a day's fun. Even ordinary working days were not always hard. Many people went regularly to the local music hall to enjoy variety concerts and shows, and by 1913 the cinema had become popular and cheap. Thousands enjoyed the make-believe world of the old silent films. Lots of people also enjoyed sport—dog-racing, pitch-and-toss, athletics, swimming, sometimes cycling and always football.

Unskilled workers were less fortunate. They generally earned less than £1 a week and lived in overcrowded back-to-back slums in the smoky parts of towns. Poverty led to disease and undernourishment. Few families could pay for a doctor or afford more than tea to drink and bread and dripping to eat. As a result, many children suffered from rickets, scurvy, tuberculosis and other illnesses caused or made worse by a poor diet. They also ran about in cast-off adult clothes, often barefoot, with head lice, poor eyesight and bad teeth. Meanwhile their parents worked long hours in mills, factories and mines. In 1900 British industry was thriving. Britain was the 'workshop of the world', but to be an unskilled industrial worker meant heat, dust, noise and grime, six days a week.

It is a harsh picture of working life, but to be unemployed was even worse. In 1900 redundancy, seasonal work, illness, old age or injury could all leave people unemployed and destitute. There was no social security system then, so when everything had been pawned (there were over 600 pawnshops in London alone)

A backstreet slum in the East End of London, 1912. Barefoot children crowd round a baker's cart. Notice the cobbled street and the tiny workers' houses. Most of the boys are wearing caps and waistcoats, just like adults, and several girls are wearing smocks

and not a penny remained, the only means of survival was either charity from the Church or Salvation Army, or else the dreaded Parish Workhouse. Here you received basic food and bedding to keep you alive, but you might also be separated from your family or have boring, unpleasant work to do, such as breaking stones. Even the lowest paid job was better, and people only went to the workhouse as a very last resort.

The new Liberal government elected in 1906 tried hard to deal with the great working-class problems of poverty and hardship, and by 1914 the gloomy picture had improved. David Lloyd George, the Chancellor of the Exchequer, had been a working-class boy himself and had seen poverty. He was particularly determined to remove 'the shadow of the workhouse from the houses of the poor', as he said. As early as 1906 the Provision of Meals Act gave free school

meals to thousands of poorer children, while the Workmen's Compensation Act forced employers to pay compensation to people injured at work. Then in 1908 the Old Age Pensions Act introduced pensions for the very first time. To begin with these were for people aged over seventy, and were fixed at a maximum of five shillings a week for single people and seven shillings and sixpence for married couples. It was not much, but it eased the fear of growing old and having no work.

Then in 1909 Lloyd George introduced the famous 'People's Budget'. It proposed to raise money to help the poor by having a tax on petrol and a road tax, an increase in income tax with an extra-heavy 'super-tax' for the rich, increased taxes on drink and tobacco, and taxes on profits made by selling or renting land. Not surprisingly there was an outcry from the

3

wealthy, many of them in the House of Lords, but Lloyd George was determined to keep up the 'war against poverty' and eventually, after a terrific struggle, the budget was passed by Parliament.

With the additional money, more schemes to help the poor now became law. In 1910 the first eighty-three labour exchanges were opened, to help people find work. In 1911 the important National Health Insurance Act was passed.

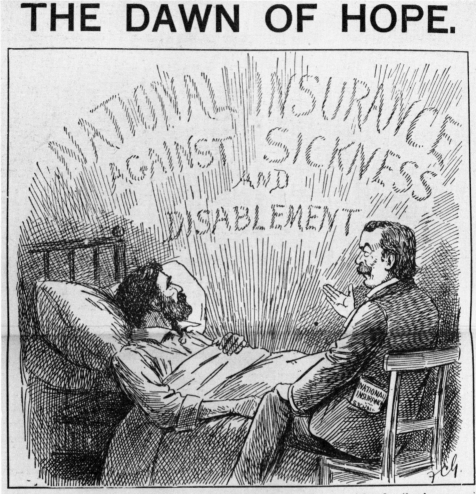

THE DAWN OF HOPE.

Mr. LLOYD GEORGE'S National Health Insurance Bill provides for the insurance of the Worker in case of Sickness.

Support the Liberal Government
in their policy of
SOCIAL REFORM.

A poster proclaiming the National Health Insurance Scheme of 1911. Lloyd George sits by the bed of a sick worker, explaining that he need never worry about being sick and off work again

The Transport Strike of 1912. The police are escorting cold-storage meat vans through London. With the city facing starvation because of the strike, the government intervened to bring food to the hungry. Later the strike failed

This was in two parts. One part protected sick workers. Each week workers paid four (old) pence into a fund. Their employers paid three-pence and the government paid two pence —'ninepence for fourpence', as they said. If a worker then fell sick, he could claim benefit of ten shillings a week for up to four months. This removed the fear of being sick and unable to support the family. The second part of the Act provided benefit for people in seasonal jobs such as shipbuilding, construction or textiles. These workers were often laid off when work was slack and only re-employed when work picked up again, but now they would receive money while out of work.

By 1914 the government had done a good deal to help the old, the sick and the unemployed. Life for many was still hard, and pawn shops and workhouses remained a common sight for many more years. Nevertheless, the Liberal reforms had gone a long way towards creating the Welfare State of today.

Changing politics

Despite the efforts made by the Liberals to improve working-class conditions, many people thought it a disgrace that such poverty and hardship should exist in a prosperous, thriving country like Britain. For many the answer was the growing trade union movement.

Previously, unions had attracted only skilled workers. But now new unions began to appear, offering unskilled people the chance to band together to press for better wages and working conditions. As a result trade union membership jumped from about 2 million in 1900 to around 6½ million in 1918.

There were several big strikes during the Edwardian period as these new unions tested their strength against employers. The engineers, dockers, transport workers and miners all staged long and bitter strikes, and often the government was forced to step in and help find a solution. What made workers so angry

5

was that while Britain's trade and industry were booming, wages and conditions were not improving. Soon the miners, railwaymen and transport workers planned to form a 'triple alliance' with the aim of having a huge general strike in 1914 to obtain better conditions for once and for all. But then the First World War began and these plans were postponed.

Trade unions were not enough, however. Many people wanted a voice in Parliament, a political party which would help them, for neither the Conservatives nor the Liberals really represented working-class feelings. In 1893 the Independent Labour Party was formed and soon the first three MPs were elected to Parliament. Later the name changed to the Labour Party. The first chairman was Keir Hardie and the first secretary was Ramsay MacDonald, both Scotsmen. With help from trade union funds, the party grew bigger. In the 1906 election, while the Liberals won easily, the Labour Party grew to twenty-nine MPs (with another twenty-four 'Lib-Lab' MPs). This increased to forty in the 1910 election as more and more working people supported the party. This was the start of the Labour Party's rise to the important position it holds today. In 1924 Ramsay MacDonald became the first Labour Prime Minister.

The Suffragettes

In 1900, many men, even in the working class, were entitled to vote in elections, but women had no vote at all. As a result, the period from 1900 to 1914 saw a determined campaign by women of all classes to win the suffrage, or right to vote. These women were called Suffragettes, a nickname given them by the *Daily Mail*.

The leaders of the Suffragette campaign were Mrs Emmeline Pankhurst and her daughers, Sylvia and Christabel. In 1903 Mrs Pankhurst founded the Women's Social and Political Union (WSPU). It quickly grew into a powerful voice, partly through its newspaper *Votes for Women*, but also as a result of the many huge meetings, demonstrations and parades which were held all over Britain. Mrs Pankhurst was an especially good public speaker. She was slim

and beautiful. She was also very brave, and was sometimes beaten and kicked at meetings. Her example inspired other women and soon a remarkable mixture of people began to help the Pankhursts organise the Suffragettes. They included Annie Kenney, a cotton-mill worker, Theresa Billington, a school-teacher, Lady Constance Lytton, and Mrs Charlotte Despard, a well-known novelist of that time.

To begin with, the Suffragettes simply held meetings and demonstrations, but when they realised that the Liberal government, elected in 1906, would not give women the vote, they changed their tactics. Women constantly interrupted government ministers at meetings, or pestered them endlessly at home, on their way to work, during election rallies and even on holiday. The slogan 'votes for women' appeared everywhere on banners and placards, even painted on walls or burned with acid onto golf courses.

As the campaign stepped up, hundreds of women chained themselves to the railings outside the Houses of Parliament, Downing Street and Buckingham Palace and had to be cut free by the police, who then arrested them. They threw stones through MPs' windows, poured acid into letter-boxes, cut telegraph wires, slashed famous paintings and set buildings on fire (but never when people were inside). In 1912 the Suffragettes smashed the windows of London's most exclusive shops in Regent Street, Oxford Street and Knightsbridge—one newspaper said that for a quarter of an hour nothing could be heard but the sound of falling, shattered glass, broken with toffee hammers and stones. Then in 1913, as some women were beginning to feel they would never succeed, Emily Davison deliberately threw herself in front of Amner, the King's horse, in the Derby. She died a few days later. Film of the incident was shown in cinemas all over the country, but it was a drastic way of gaining publicity.

Suffragette violence and vandalism soon led to jail sentences, and hundreds of normally respectable women were sent to prison. Most had never imagined that they would ever wear rough prison clothes or sleep on a mattress in a cold cell. Many continued to win publicity by

Suffragettes being arrested at a demonstration outside Buckingham Palace, May 1914

now going on hunger strikes. This led to force-feeding. Several wardresses would hold the struggling victim down while a rubber tube was pushed down into her stomach. Liquid foods such as beef tea were then poured through a funnel and down the tube. The public were shocked at this treatment of women (normally used only on certain lunatics) and this probably gained them more sympathy than anything else.

Criticism of force-feeding compelled the government to introduce the Prisoners (Temporary Discharge) Act in 1913. This allowed prison governors to release starving women for one week, and then to have them arrested again to complete their sentence. To many, this was like a cat playing with a mouse, letting it go for a moment but always dragging it back for more punishment, and the Act was soon nicknamed the 'Cat and Mouse Act'.

Despite all the publicity and the sympathy people felt for the Suffragettes, they still had not gained the vote when war began in 1914. It was difficult for politicians to support vandals and fire bombers. By 1918, however, women had won their struggle. How they did so is explained on page 100.

Ireland

Another difficult problem was Ireland. The majority of Irish people were Catholic, mostly poor peasant farmers paying high rents to English landowners. For centuries they had been poorly treated by Britain and many had emigrated to America to escape the dreadful poverty of life in Ireland. By 1900 the Catholic Irish were demanding complete independence or Home Rule. In 1905 the Sinn Fein political party was founded specifically to gain Irish freedom. Eventually the Liberals produced an Irish Home Rule Bill, which proposed an Irish Parliament, but with defence, trade and foreign affairs controlled by Parliament at Westminster.

Huge crowds in Belfast make their way to the City Hall to sign the Ulster Covenant in September 1912

The northern part of Ireland, called Ulster, was inhabited mainly by Protestants who strongly opposed this Home Rule plan, fearing that their wishes would be ignored by the larger number of Catholics. They were also more prosperous, because most Irish industry was in the north, and they feared that Catholics would get their jobs. Led by Sir Edward Carson, they formed a private army called the Ulster Volunteers to resist Home Rule. In 1912 a huge demonstration in Belfast showed how many Protestants supported Carson. Over 200,000 signed an Ulster Covenant that day, pledging opposition to Irish independence. With both sides now arming themselves, it seemed that the Liberals would soon have an Irish civil war to deal with. But in 1914 the First World War broke out, and for the moment rivalries were laid aside.

In 1916 there was a serious rebellion in Dublin (page 96). Although this caused much destruction and death in the city it did not spread to Irish troops in the British Army. All through the war, Catholic and Protestant Irishmen fought loyally for Britain and the 'Irish problem' did not reappear until the end of the war in 1918. Eventually, after much bitter fighting, a solution was found by splitting Ireland in two. Ulster was kept as part of Britain while the rest of Ireland, now called Eire, was given complete independence in 1922. Many people disagreed with this division of Ireland, and there has continued to be trouble in Ulster to the present day.

When war came in 1914 many people did not realise what a terrible struggle it would be. To people in Britain, the problems of Ireland, the Suffragettes, trade union strikes and the hardships of working-class life seemed to be the most important issues. The problems brewing in Europe, which were to cause the First World War, did not seem to be so significant.

2 The Causes of the War

Why do people fight one another? There is always a reason—something that turns one person against another until they become so angry that an argument begins, which leads to a fight. Nations are not so very different, and this chapter explains why the various countries in Europe quarrelled and finally went to war.

To begin with, we should look at the background causes of the war. These did not actually start the fighting, but they explain why the various nations were on bad terms with one another. There are six important reasons.

(1) Empire rivalry

In 1914 Russia, Germany, Austria-Hungary, France and Britain all controlled very large and powerful empires, ruling over millions of people all over the world. Even less important nations like Turkey, Holland, Portugal, Belgium and

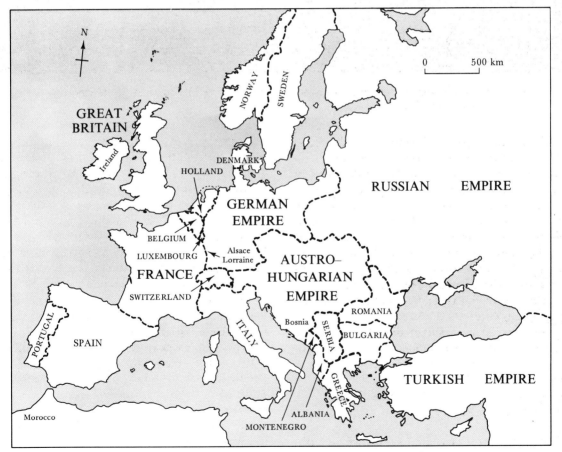

The countries of Europe in 1914

Italy had colonies, for every European state wanted to keep up with its rivals.

In any case, colonies were very useful. They provided cheap materials for the motherland's industries, food for her people, and a guaranteed market for goods from her factories. They also made the motherland look important, thereby adding to her status among other nations.

Britain undoubtedly had the greatest empire of all, spreading over Canada and the West Indies, Asia, India, Australia, New Zealand and the Pacific Ocean. More recently, nineteenth-century British explorers had opened up the 'Dark Continent' of Africa, which had started a rush by many nations to grab what they could. In the 'scramble for Africa' Britain had won almost all the best, most profitable, areas leaving the French and Italians the useless Sahara Desert, and the Germans a few large but mostly unimportant colonies. By 1914 Britain ruled over about one-quarter of the entire world. Other nations were very jealous.

France probably had the second biggest empire, and there was great rivalry as the two countries swallowed up more and more of Africa. Sometimes this nearly caused war but it was always avoided.

Germany, on the other hand, was a very new country, anxious to join the 'Great Powers' of Europe. Until 1870 she had been only a loose collection of German-speaking kingdoms and small states. Now they were united as one country, eagerly building up an army and navy and strong industries—and an empire, like every other powerful nation. The Germans were bitter. They were too late to acquire much of an empire, and by 1914 their collection of scattered colonies in Africa and the Pacific Ocean did not look very impressive. Empire rivalry was one important cause of jealousy between European nations, in particular Britain, France and Germany.

(2) Trade rivalry

Since the Germans had failed to win an impressive empire, they now hoped to become powerful world traders. Most nations controlled trade with their own colonies, but there were still some parts of the world where nations could compete for trade, such as South America, where there were fortunes to be made building railways, factories and harbours, and China, where Western nations were anxious to sell their manufactured goods to a huge population. Most European nations were involved in this worldwide rivalry over trade, but once again most attention seemed to centre on Germany and Britain. Both did very well in South America, and both had trading missions in China, but they were nevertheless rivals.

In addition, some less advanced nations were now looking for advice on how to modernise their armed forces. Both Japan and Turkey, for example, wanted to build a modern fleet of warships and re-equip their troops with new guns. Here was another opportunity to make a fortune, especially in manufacturing the new weapons. Once again Britain and Germany were the main rivals. Although Britain won some warship contracts, Germany did better. Trade rivalry was therefore a second cause of trouble, particularly between Britain and Germany.

(3) The Berlin-Baghdad Railway

One particular trade success by Germany caused more than usual anger in Britain. Turkey, although possessing an empire, was really very backward, lacking industrial knowledge and skill. Germany won a contract to build a railway through the Turkish Empire to Baghdad. This linked with a line which ran from Berlin in Germany, through the Austro-Hungarian Empire and Bulgaria to Turkey, and the whole scheme was soon called the Berlin-Baghdad Railway.

Although Germany hoped to win further trade orders as a result of constructing this track, it was not intended as a threat to anyone. In Britain, however, although the government was not worried, the public reacted strongly to the work, believing it to be some kind of sinister German plot. The line threatened British-owned oilfields in Persia, they argued—some

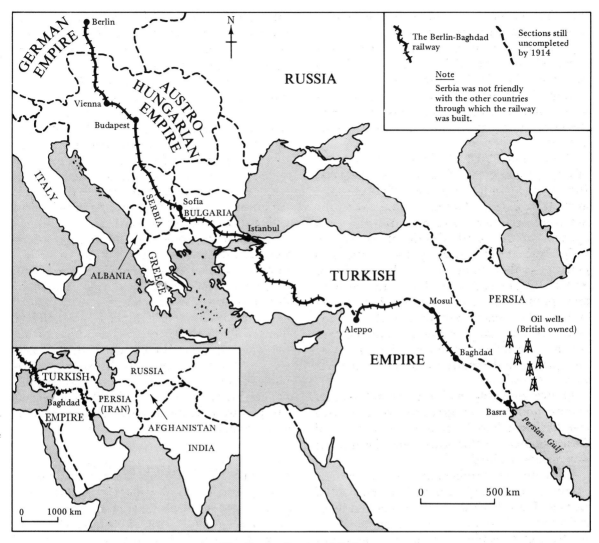

The Berlin–Baghdad Railway

even said that Baghdad could be a jumping-off place for an attack on India! It is clear now that the railway was harmless, but it made the British public angry and so added fuel to the growing quarrel between Britain and Germany.

(4) The naval arms race

The question of the Berlin-Baghdad Railway was fairly unimportant, and by itself would never have started a war. Unfortunately there was another, much more serious, problem brewing between Britain and Germany. This was the question of their rival navies.

Ever since 1805, when Admiral Nelson had defeated the French and Spanish fleets at Trafalgar, Britain had been the world's greatest sea power. The huge British Empire, and the large merchant fleet which carried British goods around the world, were so well protected by the Royal Navy that often the appearance of the only one tiny British gunboat was enough to stop trouble anywhere. Britain did indeed 'rule the waves', as the song said.

In 1873 the newly formed German nation

HMS Dreadnought

began a small programme of building warships. Then in 1895 the Germans opened the Kiel Canal, giving their ports in the Baltic Sea a quicker route to the North Sea. The British saw this as a threat, for many of Germany's battleships were normally stationed at Baltic ports—the canal was obviously designed to let these warships attack the Royal Navy, they said.

In 1898 Germany went further, and passed a law for the building of still more battleships. By 1903 Germany had as many battleships as France (thirty-six) although Britain was still far ahead with sixty-three. Nevertheless, Britain's newspapers were worried—why did the Germans need such a huge fleet, unless it was to attack the British Navy? Germany did not have

a big enough empire to justify so many ships. As a result, in 1904 a new man was put in charge of Britain's Navy, with orders to modernise it because of the German threat. His name was Admiral Sir John Fisher—Jackie Fisher to the public. By 1904, therefore, the so-called naval arms race, the race to build warships, had begun.

Fisher decided to overhaul the Navy completely. Dartmouth Naval College was founded. Old warships were scrapped. Fleets stationed overseas were brought home, leaving only a Far Eastern Squadron in Singapore. The speed with which the fleet could be got ready for action was improved. And most important of all, a completely new type of battleship was designed. This was HMS *Dreadnought*.

Launched in February 1906 and completed in the following December, *Dreadnought* made all existing battleships, including those so recently built by Britain and Germany, instantly obsolete. Its modern turbine engines made it faster than any other battleship. Its thicker armour plating gave more protection. Perhaps most important of all, *Dreadnought* had ten massive 12-inch guns in revolving turrets at each end, which enabled it to fire salvoes of shells in any direction without changing course. Moreover, the shells could travel over 11 kilometres—much farther than the smaller guns of previous battleships. Older ships could only fire a maximum of four big guns in any one direction because most guns were placed along the sides of the vessel. Thus *Dreadnought* could fight two older vessels with a gun advantage of ten to eight and sink them both before they even came in range to fire back. If they turned to escape it could catch them and sink them anyway.

Many people criticised Fisher for launching *Dreadnought*, for it made all the other British battleships just as obsolete as any others, and it no longer mattered that Britain had more than Germany. But Fisher could see that the smaller guns carried by older warships were out of date. Torpedoes now made it dangerous to get too close to the enemy, so battles would be fought at long range, using only bigger guns.

Later, more warships were built to the same plan as *Dreadnought*, and they were all known as dreadnoughts. Some dreadnoughts were built with slightly thinner armour plating, making them lighter and therefore faster. They were called dreadnought battle-cruisers, but even they could destroy any older battleship.

The launching of *Dreadnought* naturally prompted the Germans to build dreadnoughts too, and a new phase in the naval arms race began as both countries strove to create a bigger fleet of dreadnoughts than the other. The table shows how the race went. Of course, this became a major cause of distrust between Britain and Germany. Britain believed that Germany threatened the Royal Navy, while Germany felt that Britain was opposing her ambition to become a great power.

Date	Britain	Germany
1906	1	0
1907	3	0
1908	2	4
1909	2	3
1910	3	1
1911	5	3
1912	3	2
1913	7	3
1914	3	1
	—	—
Total	29	17

The race to build dreadnoughts, 1906–1914

(5) Alsace and Lorraine

So far most of the background causes of tension between nations we have considered seem to have involved Britain and Germany, but as you probably know already, France was involved in the First World War as well. Why was France hostile to Germany?

In 1870 Germany was not a united country, but consisted of a number of smaller states and kingdoms. The most powerful was Prussia, and in 1870 the Prussians attacked France. In a bitter war which caused serious starvation in Paris, the French were easily defeated and their emperor was captured. The mighty French Empire was humiliated by a small German kingdom. Then, to make matters worse, the French were required to sign the peace treaty in the Hall of Mirrors at Versailles, the famous royal palace just outside Paris. Here the Germans demanded that the French give up two important border provinces, Alsace and Lorraine. This was a blow to France, for these two regions were rich in coal and iron, on which French industry depended. But as a defeated nation the French could only do as the Prussians demanded. A few months later Germany was united into one country and the King of Prussia became the Emperor of Germany, which now included Alsace and Lorraine.

Defeat in the Franco-Prussian War, and the

loss of these two important provinces, left the French determined to win back their territory from the Germans. Soon the French Army was expanded, and most of it was stationed along the German frontier as if waiting for an opportunity to attack. The Germans reacted by doing the same, and soon thousands of soldiers faced each other across the border. The loss of Alsace and Lorraine was clearly a very important cause of tension between France and Germany.

(6) Russia and 'Pan-Slavism'

Meanwhile a separate quarrel was building up at the other end of Europe between Russia, Austria-Hungary and Turkey. The Turks, and more especially the Austrians, ruled over millions of people of different races. The map shows many separate races all ruled over by the German-speaking Austrians or the Turks. These minority peoples had little say in their own affairs. Their languages and customs were often outlawed and their newspapers closed down. People of different religions were persecuted, especially by the Turks. They had no vote and could not hold important jobs. Little wonder that these minorities hated their rulers and longed for freedom to govern themselves.

That freedom was not as hopeless a dream as it seemed. Almost all the minority peoples were Slavs, like the Russians. Here was an excellent excuse for the mighty Russian Empire to gain some prestige at the expense of the Austrians and Turks. The Russians supported these minorities and demanded better conditions for them.

Soon the Croats, Czechs and other Slavs regarded Russia as a protector and friend. Russia did not really care very much for her Slav brothers—the minorities served mainly as an excuse, as Russia tried to dominate her two neighbouring rival empires. But the minority peoples did not realise this, and the idea of all Slavs being brothers (known as 'Pan-Slavism') produced a new wave of demands, for newspapers in Slavonic languages and so on. In the Turkish Empire many Slavs even fought in open rebellion against the cruel rule of the Sultans.

Turkey and Austria both blamed their troubles on Russia, for encouraging the Slavs to rebel, and this caused great tension. The question of Pan-Slavism therefore helped to spread the quarrel among Europe's leading nations.

Two armed camps

Out of this mixture of quarrelling nations, two sides gradually formed. Germany felt very isolated. Britain and France were clearly against her, as she struggled to establish a place among the great European empires. As a result Germany formed an alliance in 1879 with the Austro-Hungarian Empire, in which each side promised to help the other in the event of war. In 1882 Italy, another nation looking for glory and power, joined these two, thus creating the Triple Alliance, sometimes called the Central Powers. This suited them all, for Austria could face up to Russia knowing that she had an ally, while the Germans could stop worrying about Britain or France, for neither of them would attack, knowing that it would also mean war with Austria and Italy.

This defensive arrangement seemed to offer safety for the Triple Alliance, but then the plan went wrong. In 1894 France made an unexpected treaty with her old enemy Russia. As with the German-Austrian alliance, this also said that if either nation was attacked, the other would help. Now the Triple Alliance was sandwiched between France and Russia.

Meanwhile Britain stood aside from all this treaty-making. She disliked France and Russia as much as Germany, and so preferred to carry on alone, in splendid isolation. However, as Germany became part of the Triple Alliance the British needed to have some friends after all, and reluctantly looked around for a suitable ally. The French and Russians were out of the question—they were rivals, not friends. At the same time most other nations disapproved of Britain because of the war—the Boer War—which she was fighting against the Dutch farmers of South Africa (a war which included burning farms and keeping prisoners in concentration camps). The world supported the underdogs against the bully, which made it

Area where Slavs lived

Notice the large number of Slav peoples living in Austria-Hungary.

Most Slavs in the Turkish Empire were free by 1914, e.g. Bulgarians, Serbs.

Notice also the Arabs and Armenians in Turkey.

The minority peoples in Austria and Turkey

hard for Britain to find an ally at that moment. However there was one friend: in 1902 Britain signed a treaty with Japan. It was the start of a new era as Britain realised the need for allies.

Then in 1904 Britain agreed to stop quarrell-ing with France. They settled their differences over numerous colonies and promised not to overlap in finding new colonies. This arrange-ment was known as the *Entente Cordiale* or friendly agreement—it was not a promise to go

15

The German Army practising battle manoeuvres in 1912. Scenes like this made the French very suspicious of the Germans

to war to help each other, but it did give both countries some confidence against their common enemy, Germany.

In 1907 Britain made a similar agreement with Russia, and the Triple Entente was created. Again, although France and Russia were firm allies, there was no obligation on Britain to fight with them in any war. Nevertheless, by 1907 it was clear that out of the mixture of quarrelling empires, two sides had been created.

Both groups, the Triple Alliance and the Triple Entente, now began to add to their weapons. The British and the Germans were racing to build dreadnought battleships. At the same time the French and the Germans had huge armies facing each other across the borders of Alsace and Lorraine. The Russians and

the Austro-Hungarians also had huge armies. Even the Turks had a large army, recently modernised by the Germans, while the Japanese had new warships, many built by Britain. Meanwhile the small British Army was improved by R. B. Haldane, the Secretary of State for War. His important reforms included having the troops ready for immediate travel to any trouble spot, should a war begin, and also the creation of the Territorial Army, made up of well-trained civilian volunteers, as a reserve for the professional army. So there were two enemy camps, both heavily armed. Each side expected a war to settle a quarrel with some nation on the other side. Each side believed that, with its allies, it was bound to win. All they needed was an excuse to start fighting.

Four incidents gradually led to World War

One. They could be called the immediate causes of the war. Three times the world nearly came to blows, but tempers cooled and peace survived. On the fourth occasion the war began.

The First Moroccan Crisis, 1905

The French were generally recognised as the major European power in Morocco, in North Africa, but they were having difficulty in controlling the area. In 1905, the German ruler, Kaiser Wilhelm II, made a visit to the Moroccan port of Tangier. In a speech he declared Germany's support for the Moroccans. The Germans saw this as a chance to score a diplomatic success, and to prove that they were just as important now as France. The French, of course, were furious with the Germans for meddling in a private French colonial problem which had nothing to do with the Kaiser.

War between France and Germany was avoided by the calling of an international conference, which was held at Algeçiras in southern Spain. Here France was supported by Britain and the USA in condemning the Germans for interfering in Morocco. The Germans were outvoted and went home utterly humiliated. For the Kaiser, Wilhelm II, it was also a personal blow. He had a slightly withered left arm, caused by a careless midwife at his birth, and he made up for this by swaggering about wearing impressive uniforms (see page 108). His ambition to be seen as the ruler of a powerful empire was crushed by the conference at Algeçiras. When a country or its leader feels bitter and humiliated, the possibility of war next time is increased.

The Bosnian Crisis, 1908

As we have seen, the Austrians and Turks both ruled over Slav peoples whom they treated very unfairly. By 1900 feelings of Pan-Slavism had grown into constant trouble, especially in the Turkish Empire, which was not very powerful. This part of Europe was called the Balkans, and so the Slav demands for freedom became known as the Balkan Question.

One remote corner of the Turkish Empire was called Bosnia. As elsewhere, the Slav people here longed for independence and had been fighting a terrorist war against Turkey for years. Their neighbour, Serbia, had already succeeded, and it seemed only a matter of time before the Bosnians became such a nuisance to Turkey that they would also be given their freedom. Already Turkish rule in Bosnia was so feeble that Austria, to the north, was actually ruling over much of the area.

In 1908 the Turks finally gave up Bosnia, but instead of granting independence, they transferred the entire province to Austria. The Bosnians, so close to success, were horrified, for Austrian rule was no better than Turkish rule. They begged the Russians to help their Slav brothers, but Russia was not yet ready to fight in 1908, having just lost a war against Japan in 1905. In addition, the Germans loudly supported their Austrian allies, so Russia kept quiet and Bosnia was swallowed up into the Austro-Hungarian Empire. But the Bosnian people had a deep hatred of Austria, and were bitterly disappointed in Russia. If the Russians wanted to continue as the protector of minority Slav peoples, they would have to help next time.

The Second Moroccan Crisis, 1911

In July 1911 the German warship *Panther* appeared in the Moroccan port of Agadir. This angered the French, who remembered the previous Moroccan Crisis in 1905. But it also worried the British, who believed the Germans wanted to establish a naval base at Agadir, close to the vital British base at Gibraltar.

The British Chancellor of the Exchequer, Lloyd George, in a speech at the Mansion House in London, clearly warned the Germans to pull out of Agadir, or else it would mean war. (Remember that Britain and Germany were already suspicious of each other.) To Germany, this was more proof that Britain did not want her to join the other great powers in Europe. To the British it was evidence that the German Navy intended to threaten the Royal Navy. But was it worth a war?

The Archduke Franz Ferdinand (left) and his wife Sophie arrive at Sarajevo on the day of their murder

Eventually the Germans gave way, realising that Britain and France were united over this matter and that a war would be a terrible price to pay for an unimportant seaport. Once again the world watched the Germans being humiliated as they gave in. More important, this crisis helped strengthen the recently formed friendship between Britain and France, making it more likely that Britain would fight with France in any future war.

The murder at Sarajevo, 1914

The burning hatred of the Slav peoples for their Austrian rulers reached a peak in 1914. The Bosnian Crisis of 1908, when the province was transferred to Austrian rule, was the breaking point. The Serbians, who were already independent, now encouraged their Bosnian neighbours to fight. A secret society called the Black Hand was formed, consisting of Bosnian terrorists who were trained and given weapons over the mountains in Serbia. By 1914 the Black Hand had already assassinated several important Austrian officials in Bosnia.

Despite this, the Austrian Archduke, Franz Ferdinand, decided to visit the troubled province. In particular he wanted a royal procession through the streets of Sarajevo, the capital of Bosnia. As he was first in line for the royal throne (the elderly Franz Josef was Emperor), it was a risky visit and the Archduke became an obvious target—a much better victim for the

Black Hand than mere local officials. An attack was soon being plotted in neighbouring Serbia.

It was never difficult to find terrorist volunteers in Bosnia, for there were many students and young men eager to fight the Austrians. Soon Danilo Ilic, the Black Hand's agent in Sarajevo, found six keen young men for the job. Two were still only schoolboys and two more were still teenagers, but they were all dedicated to freedom for Bosnia. The most reliable of the six was Gavrilo Princip, the son of a postman. Aged nineteen, he was intelligent, bitterly anti-Austrian, and a fanatical Bosnian. Soon the six were learning from Ilic about bombs and pistols in a railway tunnel near Sarajevo. Then at last the day came.

Sunday 28 June 1914 was bright and sunny. Sarajevo had been specially decked out for the royal visit and colourful Turkish rugs hung from balconies along the route. Tall poplar trees lined the riverside road and bright flowers grew everywhere. Crowds lined the streets and waited for the procession of cars to appear. Of course the Archduke had been warned that the city was full of Bosnian nationalists sworn to kill him, but the procession went ahead as planned. The Archduke had received so many death threats in the past that now he just courageously ignored them.

Meanwhile the six terrorists were stationed at intervals along the Appel Quay—the riverside route which the cars would follow on their way to the Town Hall. Two waited at the Hungarian Bank and two more across the road by the Cumurja Bridge, with Princip at the Lateiner Bridge and Grabez further on at the Kaiser Bridge. They all had bombs and pistols in their pockets, and phials of poison which

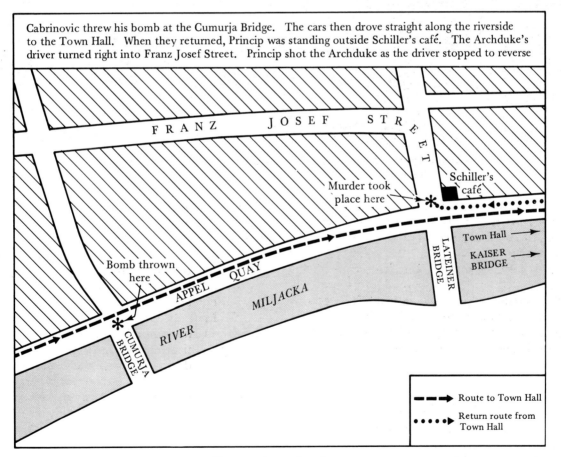

The murder at Sarajevo

they had promised to swallow if they were caught, so that they would not give the others away. It seemed as if the plan could not fail. One of them was bound to kill the Archduke.

Finally the cavalcade of four large cars came into sight. The mayor of Sarajevo came first, followed by the Archduke in a green open-topped car. He looked every inch a duke, wearing a pale blue uniform, a row of glittering medals and a military hat decorated with green ostrich feathers. Beside him sat his wife Sophie, looking beautiful in a white dress and a broad hat and waving politely to the crowd. In front sat the local governor, General Potiorek, and Count Harrach, the car's owner, both worried for their royal guests.

At 10.15 the cars passed Mehmedbasic, the first in line of the waiting killers. He took fright, did nothing, and then escaped. Nearby the next assassin, a schoolboy called Cabrilovic, also lost his nerve and did nothing. But then as the cars passed the Cumurja Bridge, Cabrinovic threw his bomb, swallowed his poison, and jumped into the river. The Archduke saw the bomb coming and threw it off his car, but it exploded under the car behind, injuring several people. Now there was total confusion as the procession accelerated away, fearing more bombs. Meanwhile the police dragged Cabrinovic out of the river. His cyanide was old and had not worked.

The Archduke was driven to the Town Hall, where he demanded to be taken to visit the bomb victims in hospital. Fearing more terrorists, the officials decided to take a new route to avoid the crowds, but this was not properly explained to the driver of the Archduke's car. Moreover, no police guard went with the procession.

Meanwhile the other assassins, on hearing the bomb explode, assumed the Archduke was dead and left—all except Princip, who soon discovered the truth. Miserably he wandered across the street towards Schiller's delicatessen and café.

Princip was standing outside the café when, at 10.45, the Archduke's car suddenly appeared beside him and turned into Franz Josef Street. This was a mistake, for according to the new plan the procession should have continued straight along the Appel Quay. As the driver realised he had taken a wrong turn he stopped and started to reverse. Princip could hardly believe his luck. Pulling an automatic pistol from the right-hand pocket of his coat, he fired two shots at a range of just 3 or 4 metres. He could not miss. One bullet pierced the Archduke's neck and the other, meant for General Potiorek, ricocheted off the car into Sophie's stomach. She slumped across her husband, who gasped, 'Sophie! Don't die. Stay alive for our children.' But fifteen minutes later she died and the Archduke followed soon after.

Princip was immediately seized. Although he managed to swallow his poison, it did not work and he was taken off to prison. All the plotters except Mehmedbasic were eventually caught, but only the organiser, Ilic, was hanged, for the others were too young for the death penalty. Princip died in an Austrian jail, however, in April 1918, aged twenty-three.

The murder of the Archduke had a shattering effect on Europe. Within five weeks the world was at war and the slaughter of 10 million soldiers had begun. Princip later said that if he had known what was to follow he would never have fired the two fatal shots—but his regret was too late.

3 Europe Rushes into War

By 1914 all the powerful nations of Europe were resigned to the prospect of war. They could not know what a terrible war it would be, but the two sides felt powerful and confident as their huge armies and navies manoeuvered and trained for battle. Meanwhile, suspicion and hatred deepened and war drew closer.

The Germans, who were ruled by Kaiser Wilhelm II, had suffered particularly. Germany, a new European nation, wanted instant power and importance, but she was losing the race with Britain to build dreadnoughts, her empire was not impressive, and she had twice been humiliated for interfering in Morocco. Not surprisingly, the patriotic Germans and their Kaiser were seeking revenge.

The French, already bitter at having lost Alsace and Lorraine to Germany, had been building up a huge army which by 1914 had over 4 million men. In addition, the two crises over Morocco had deepened French dislike of Germany. Now, with British and Russian support, the French were ready for war.

The Russians, who had done nothing to help the Bosnians in 1908, needed a second chance to show their support for the minority Slavs. If they did not help this time, Russia's importance as a protector would disappear. Meanwhile Austria was looking for a chance to crush the rebellious Slav peoples once and for all. In particular the Austrians disliked Serbia, for this small independent Slav nation was encouraging all the others to resist Austrian (and Turkish) rule.

Britain, already a trade and empire rival of Germany, was deeply suspicious of the growing German Navy. Popular newspapers were whipping up public opinion against this threat from Germany. Now, with the two sides formed, all that was needed was an excuse to start shooting. The murder of the Archduke Franz Ferdinand at Sarajevo was that excuse.

Austria attacks Serbia

Although the murder took place in the Bosnian city of Sarajevo, and the assassins were all Bosnians, the Austrians realised that Serbia was also involved. In fact, although the Serbian government probably did not know of the plot, many senior Serbian officials, including the chief of the intelligence service, certainly did. Moreover, the guns and bombs were provided by Serbia. There was no proof, but the suspicion was good enough for Austria.

Less than a month later the Austrians sent the Serbian government an ultimatum. This was a list of ten demands, which the Serbians had to agree to within two days or else the Austrians would attack them. The Serbians bravely rejected two of the demands—that there should be Austrian officers in the Serbian Army, and Austrian ministers in the Serbian government. If the Serbs had agreed to these points their country would have become just another part of the Austro-Hungarian Empire. Of course Austria knew this. To her it was an ideal solution—either Serbia came under Austrian control, or she would be crushed in a war. Either way, it would prevent Serbia from encouraging more terrorism.

But Serbia accepted only eight of the ten demands, which was not good enough. Urged on by promises of support from Germany, the Austrians declared war on Serbia and attacked on 29 July. There was little chance of the tiny Serbian Army fighting off this invasion and desperately the Serbian government begged

21

Russia to help. It was the chance Russia had been hoping for.

The other nations declare war

One day later the Russian armies began to advance towards both the Austrian and the German borders. On 1 August Germany declared war on Russia, which immediately brought in France (remember that France and Russia had promised to help each other if either was attacked). What had started as a quarrel between Austria and Serbia had grown within a week to war between the great European empires. Although Britain was not yet involved, the Royal Navy had already been sent to its war stations at sea, for it was clear that war was coming.

The steps to war in 1914

28 June   Archduke Franz Ferdinand murdered at Sarajevo in Bosnia. Austria blames Serbia.

23 July   Austrian ultimatum to Serbia, with ten demands.

25 July   Serbia rejects two demands from the ultimatum. Germany urges Austria to attack Serbia. Serbia prepares for war.

29 July   Austria attacks Serbia.

30 July   Russia prepares for war to help Serbia.

31 July   Austria prepares for war with Russia.

1 August   Germany mobilises her troops. Germany declares war on Russia. France prepares for war.

2 August   German troops move up to the French and Belgian frontiers.

3 August   Germany declares war on France. Britain warns Germany not to attack Belgium.

4 August   Germany invades Belgium. Britain declares war on Germany.

Note It was only one week from the Austrian attack on Serbia to the invasion of Belgium and Britain joining the war. Just two days later British troops were sailing for France. Some historians have argued that there was no time to stop the war—it began so fast. Most countries, not realising what lay ahead, did not try to stop it anyway.

The Schlieffen Plan

The biggest problem for Germany was that she lay between her two enemies France and Russia. While they could attack with their full armies, the Germans would have to split theirs to fight in two directions at once. This is called 'fighting a war on two fronts'.

In 1905, since war with France could be expected one day, Count von Schlieffen, the Chief of the German General Staff, had prepared a plan to deal with the problem of a war on two fronts. Von Schlieffen said that although the Russian armies were huge, the terrible state of Russian roads and the lack of railways meant it would take at least six weeks to assemble troops from all over the vast Russian countryside. On the other hand the French were ready with a huge army for an immediate attack, especially in Alsace and Lorraine. This meant that the Germans would have six weeks during which the whole army could fight France, before the Russians arrived. If the French could be defeated in six weeks, the entire German Army could then travel east and fight the Russians. That would avoid having to split the army to fight in two directions at once. The problem was how to defeat the mighty French in just six weeks.

The entire French-German border was bristling with troops, and behind them lay a chain of heavily protected towns defended by huge underground concrete forts. Clearly it would be difficult to smash through this area in six weeks. But there was one big gap in the French defences. The Belgian frontier was undefended.

Belgium was a neutral country—the Belgians did not want to fight on any side in any war, and had made no promises to, or alliances with, anyone. Normally, warring nations respect neutral countries and leave them alone. This is why the French had no troops along their Belgian frontier, for they did not intend to fight there and did not expect a Belgian attack.

Von Schlieffen decided to attack through Belgium. The Belgian Army was small and would be easily brushed aside. Then the Germans would sweep through northern France

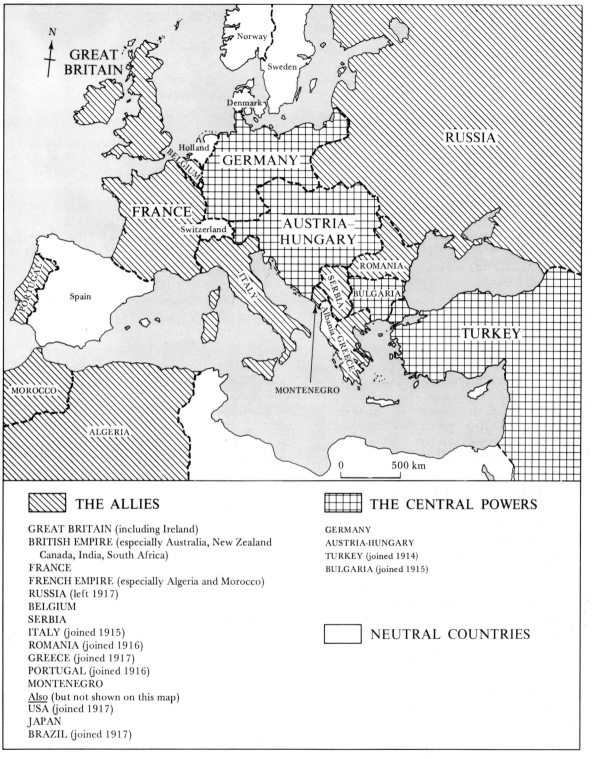

▨ **THE ALLIES**	⊞ **THE CENTRAL POWERS**
GREAT BRITAIN (including Ireland)	GERMANY
BRITISH EMPIRE (especially Australia, New Zealand Canada, India, South Africa)	AUSTRIA-HUNGARY
	TURKEY (joined 1914)
FRANCE	BULGARIA (joined 1915)
FRENCH EMPIRE (especially Algeria and Morocco)	
RUSSIA (left 1917)	
BELGIUM	
SERBIA	
ITALY (joined 1915)	▢ **NEUTRAL COUNTRIES**
ROMANIA (joined 1916)	
GREECE (joined 1917)	
PORTUGAL (joined 1916)	
MONTENEGRO	
<u>Also</u> (but not shown on this map)	
USA (joined 1917)	
JAPAN	
BRAZIL (joined 1917)	

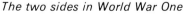

The two sides in World War One

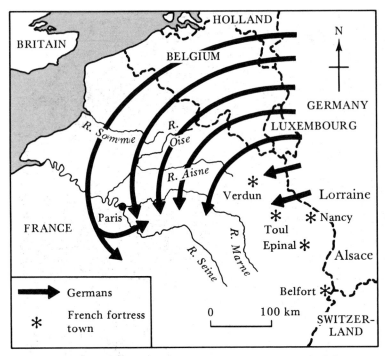

The Schlieffen Plan, 1905

with six parallel armies in an enormous curve, and surround Paris. Attacking through Belgium was a dirty trick, but it would bring victory in the vital six weeks. The French armies were expected to attack Alsace and Lorraine, obsessed with the idea of winning back these lost provinces. If the Germans moved fast enough the French would realise too late that Paris was surrounded, and they would be unable to do anything about it, as the map shows. In addition, Von Schlieffen believed that although the French would have great enthusiasm while attacking, their spirits would collapse if Paris was captured. Then France would surrender and the Germans could transfer their armies to the Russian frontier.

Britain joins the war

On 4 August the German armies poured over the Belgian frontier. In Berlin the British ambassador, Sir Edward Goschen, took a message to the German Chancellor, Herr Bethmann-Holweg. It said that if the German troops did not leave Belgium before midnight, Britain would declare war on Germany and Austria.

Why was Britain so concerned with Belgium? Many years earlier, in 1839, by the Treaty of London, Britain had promised to help defend Belgium against any attacker. At that time the possible enemy had been France, but the promise still held good in 1914 when the Germans invaded. The Germans did not believe that Britain would keep to such an old treaty, a mere 'scrap of paper', as they called it, and in London too, many politicians were uncertain about the obligation to fight for Belgium. Half of the Cabinet wanted Britain to stay neutral, so the British Foreign Secretary, Sir Edward Grey, called for a European Conference to help maintain peace. The German Kaiser rejected this, and soon German troops invaded Belgium, leaving Britain with no honourable alternative but to declare war.

In Berlin, Sir Edward Goschen knew perfectly well that the Germans could not pull out of Belgium by midnight, for they were moving to a complicated railway timetable which could not be reversed without causing great confusion. Midnight came and to no one's surprise German armies were still pouring into Belgium. By then the British ambassador and his staff were gone, and Britain declared war. 'The

When war broke out, crowds in many European cities cheered the news. This photograph shows enthusiastic Germans in Munich. Near the front, and also shown in close-up, is 25-year-old Adolf Hitler. Next day he joined the German Army. During the war he was gassed, and then wounded in 1918, for which he won a medal

efforts of a life-time go for nothing,' said a disappointed Sir Edward Grey, although in the streets, crowds cheered the news.

Why did the great powers plunge so willingly into such a terrible war? First, no one realised what was to come. Every nation believed it would win by Christmas. Second, the crisis which sparked off the fighting was too sudden to allow the normal processes of diplomacy to work. There were no aeroplanes to whisk politicians to emergency meetings. Sir Edward Grey was actually away bird-watching and could not even be contacted quickly. In any case, to most British people the Irish problem seemed more important than a murder in far-off Sarajevo. Third, both Russia and Germany had backed down in previous crises and neither was willing to do so again. Moreover, each nation saw something worth fighting for. Even the Austrians, who had not won a war for years, saw a chance of victory in an attack on Serbia.

The Battle of the Marne

Although the Schlieffen Plan had been worked out in great detail, several things now happened which the Germans had not expected. The Russians moved much faster than anyone had anticipated. Within ten days two huge Russian armies were marching into eastern Germany, and troops had to be sent from France to delay them. What happened to the Russians is explained on page 63.

The Belgians were not swept aside as easily as the Germans had expected. Deep concrete forts protecting cities like Antwerp, Liège and Namur seriously delayed the Germans. Heavy guns had to be called up to pound the defences to rubble. Even then, Antwerp did not surrender until 10 October, nine weeks after the Germans first attacked. So while the Belgians did not stop the invasion, their unexpected resistance slowed down the German advance.

Another factor which interfered with the Schlieffen Plan was the arrival of the British Army, led by General French. Unlike the other

NO THOROUGHFARE

BRAVO, BELGIUM!

A Punch *magazine cartoon of August 1914. It shows how most British people thought of the Belgians—a brave people refusing to let the big German bully through*

Troops of the BEF sail for France in August 1914. The men with flat caps are Scots Guards, and those wearing 'Glengarry bonnets' are Gordon Highlanders. Notice how many men have a moustache—a popular fashion at that time

great powers, Britain did not have a large army, preferring instead to build up a navy to defend her shores. Nevertheless a small force of 100,000 men was prepared within a week of war being declared. Surprisingly the Germans did not interfere with the troopships and within days the first British troops were in France. This army was called the British Expeditionary Force (BEF) and on 23 August it met the first Germans in a battle at the mining town of Mons. The BEF was small but it was excellently trained—the British rifle fire, for example, was so fast and accurate that the Germans believed they were facing machine-guns.

The Germans did not particularly fear the British. The Kaiser merely ordered his men to 'exterminate first the treacherous English and walk over General French's contemptible little army'. As a result, the BEF was soon nicknamed the 'Old Contemptibles'. Although the

The BEF in retreat through France. 'J' Battery of the Royal Horse Artillery passes through a French village in October 1914. Soon these men were fighting in the First Battle of Ypres (see page 30)

Army was not defeated at Mons the outnumbered British force could only delay the Germans and eventually it was pushed back into France. There was more desperate fighting at Le Cateau but gradually the British were driven back across the River Marne.

It seemed like failure for the Allies, but in fact although the Germans were still advancing, the Schlieffen Plan was in ruins. Orders and food supplies from Germany were not keeping up with the advancing armies. In addition, von Schlieffen knew that of all the German armies required for the attack through Belgium, the one at the right-hand end of the line would have to travel farthest—it was supposed to encircle Paris. He urged that this army should be six times stronger than any other, to allow for

casualties on the exhausting march round Paris. In 1913 his dying words are said to have been 'Keep the right wing strong!'. However, the siege of Antwerp and the defiant battles fought by British and Belgian troops had so delayed this army that its speed was lost and it would never reach Paris in time. Moreover a wide split had opened between this army and the one beside it, so the Germans abandoned the plan to encircle Paris, as the map opposite shows.

What had the French armies been doing? As expected, the French were interested only in Alsace and Lorraine, which they attacked without realising that the German defenders were only a decoy. The main German attack was meanwhile sweeping behind them through

Belgium, and might have succeeded had it not been for the Belgians and British. Then the French suddenly realised the trap. If they did not move quickly the armies would be cut off from Paris.

The French decided to stand and fight the Germans at the River Marne. By now some German troops were already across the river and could actually see the Eiffel Tower rising above Paris. They must have felt very close to victory. But then the French and British arrived. French troops from Alsace and Lorraine, some marching until they were exhausted, some brought by rail, now arrived at the river. Between the French armies stood the British, pushed back from Belgium but still intact. Then an extraordinary thing happened. Long queues of buses and taxis left Paris, carrying every available soldier from the city, and another makeshift French army was formed.

A terrible battle followed as exhausted foot-soldiers on both sides fought to win the war. If the Germans won, they might still defeat France and have time to fight Russia. For the French, it was a battle to save Paris. Then a British aeroplane pilot reported that a wide gap had opened between the German armies in front of the British forces. Cautiously the British advanced, and the Germans, realising the trap, pulled back to the River Aisne. Almost cetainly the Germans had already decided to retreat anyway, for their horses and men were utterly worn out from weeks of hard fighting and fast marching. On 19 September the battle ended and Paris was saved. For the French the 'Taxis of the Marne' became a legend, although British troops were actually first to cross the river again. More important, the Schlieffen Plan was in ruins. General von Kluck, commander of the army which had failed to encircle Paris, even said to the Kaiser, 'We have lost the war.'

The race to the sea

Despite their retreat from the River Marne, the Germans were not defeated, for they still occupied most of north-east France and

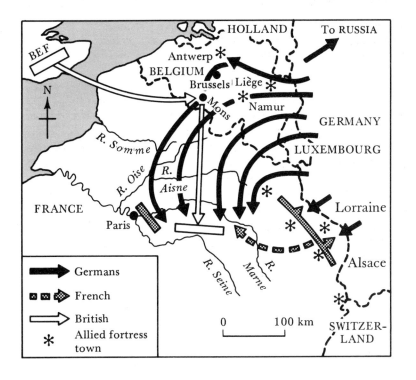

The German attack, 1914

29

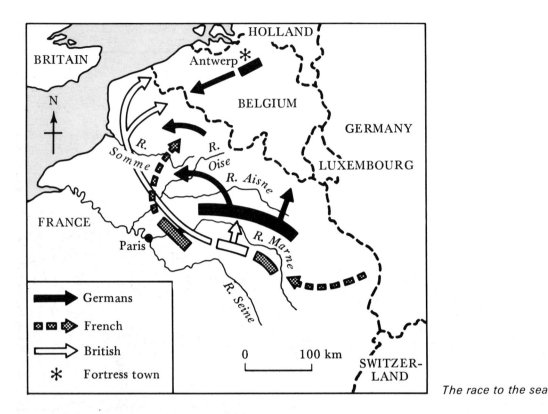

The race to the sea

Belgium. Their only hope now was to surround rapidly the French and British Armies. As the map shows, both sides had the same idea. The Germans tried to sweep round to the north, but so did the French. Realising that they had failed, the Germans tried again to outflank (go round the side of) the French, but wherever they pushed, they found the French also moving into position. Of course the French were also unable to trap the Germans.

Meanwhile the British had been pushed deep into France and realised that they were in danger of being cut off from the French ports on the English Channel which brought in their supplies. They ignored the French and Germans and made a hasty march north to prevent vital ports like Dunkirk, Calais and Boulogne from falling into German hands. They arrived in time, helped by the Belgians who deliberately flooded their countryside, just as the Germans tried one last time to curve round northwards behind the Allies. The British and Germans met in a bloody battle at the town of Ypres, where 13,000 Prussian

Guards, the very best of the German Army, attacked the British and were massacred. Bodies piled up in heaps but still the Germans kept coming. In some places the British defences broke and there was desperate hand-to-hand fighting in the woods around the town, but finally after a month the attacks ended. About 20,000 of Germany's finest troops were killed, and another 80,000 were wounded. The British had lost 8,000 but Ypres was saved and the Germans were prevented from reaching the coast. The Allies had won the race to the sea.

Christmas, 1914

So far, the fighting in France had been a story of armies manoeuvring to trap the enemy in a 'war of movement'. However the fighting at Ypres ended on 22 November, well into winter. Now movement was not so easy.

The land around Ypres was flat and muddy, churned up by heavy shelling which made it difficult to attack. Machine-guns had also

30

'E' Battery of the Royal Horse Artillery in action on 31 October 1914. The guns are small compared with the much more powerful field-guns used later in the war (see photograph on page 51)

forced everyone to take cover—what started off as hiding in a ditch became more permanent as the battle went on. 'Trenches' appeared (see Chapter 4) and the war of movement was over. There was no way round the enemy: an unbroken line of trenches soon stretched from the English Channel to the Swiss border in the south. For the next four years the war was fought from these trenches.

Christmas 1914 came—the time when soldiers on both sides had expected to come home victorious. Instead they were living in holes in the ground, bitterly cold, homesick, and with no idea when victory would come. On Christmas Day itself an extraordinary thing happened in many places. An unofficial truce began and the shooting died away. German soldiers sang carols, and from their trenches the British responded. They shouted greetings to each other, and in some places men from both sides actually climbed out of their trenches to celebrate Christmas together, swopping cigarettes and chocolate and playing football. But two days later the shooting started again and the last hope of peace disappeared.

When Christmas 1915 came, the troops were still there in the same trenches, but there were no carols, for by then everyone hated the war. What had started as a war of movement which either side might win had become a stalemate.

4 Life in the Trenches

By late 1914 trenches had appeared all along the fighting line in France and Belgium. Soon they became more or less permanent and an intricate web of additional trenches then developed, with supply railways, hospitals and kitchens, complicated defensive 'strong points' and protected paths leading to the 'front line'. These trenches became home for millions of men on both sides.

The trench system

The front line faced the enemy, who might be between 200 and 800 metres away. The space in between was called No-Man's-Land. Each side protected itself with rows of barbed wire, secretly erected or improved at night. No-Man's-Land became a deserted strip of devastated battleground, pitted by shellfire and

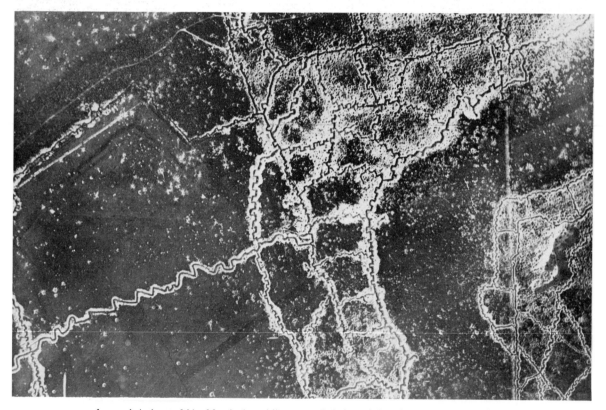

An aerial view of No-Man's-Land (bottom right) *and the zig-zag pattern of the opposing trenches. The British have dug firing bays into No-Man's-Land from their front line. Communication trenches run back to the second and third lines and then to the rear. The white marks are shell holes. Most of the shells have landed near the front line*

Men of the Yorks and Lancs Regiment in a typical trench. Two men check the drum magazine of a Lewis machine-gun. An officer peers into a periscope, which has been disguised with sacking. At the back, a soldier pours water from a petrol can into his mess-tin. Sandbags have been used to strengthen the parapet and there are duckboards along the bottom of the trench

muddy from rain. Here, shattered grey trees sometimes stood where green woods had once grown, and dead bodies lay rotting, often caught on the barbed wire.

Behind the front line were the 'reserve trenches'. These were a second line of defence in battle, in case the front line should be captured, but they were also used as a resting place for front-line troops. Sometimes the reserve trenches were known as the second line or 'support trenches'. There were even parts of a third line in some places but this was not so common.

Running across these lines were the 'communication trenches'. They led back to safety, sometimes for a kilometre or more, until they were far enough away from enemy guns. Everything going to the front or 'up the line' had to use these communication trenches—fresh troops, food, water, mail, ammunition and all other supplies. Wounded men came the other way, towards the hospitals.

The layout of a trench

Most trenches were deep enough for a man to walk without his head being seen and wide enough for a man to rest while others went by. Sometimes rocks or water-logged ground made it impossible to dig deep enough, and these trenches were more dangerous—any man showing his head even for a moment could be killed by waiting enemy snipers, so the men had to crouch all day, or crawl uncomfortably.

The soil dug out of a trench was usually

33

Men of the Border Regiment resting in dug-outs. Sandbags have been used to strengthen the walls. Some dug-outs were larger than those shown here

heaped in front to form a 'parapet' which gave extra protection from bullets. Sometimes this was reinforced with additional sandbags or anything else that was handy. The trench would also have a 'firing step', to enable the men to see over the parapet. Since it was dangerous to show your head, the firing step was generally used only by sentries at night, or in battle when the troops were shooting. The normal way of watching the enemy in safety was to use a periscope. This was a box tube with a peep-hole at the bottom and a wider space at the top, and a mirror fixed inside, carefully angled. Troops held this up over the parapet to watch enemy movements while they stayed under cover. The back walls of a trench were sometimes strengthened with railway

sleepers, corrugated iron, or specially made sections of woven basket-work fencing. These reinforcements were useless under heavy shell-fire, but they did help to stop the soil slipping down into the trench.

Wherever possible, trenches were dug in a zig-zag line. This lessened the blast from shells and prevented attackers from shooting right along a straight trench. Also, if the enemy did capture part of a trench, they would still have to fight round every corner to win the rest of it. Barbed-wire doors were placed at intervals along many trenches. When open, the doors fitted into recesses in the trench wall, but in battle they were closed in the hope of slowing down the enemy if they got into the trench. In addition to their zig-zag shape, many trenches also had 'firing bays' which pushed a few extra metres into No-Man's-Land, allowing the men to fire into the sides of the enemy as they attacked the trench.

Rain quickly made most trenches very muddy, so 'duckboards' were laid end-to-end along the bottom. These were flat planks of wood nailed together like a ladder. They did not sink into the mud and made walking easier. Duckboards soon became a common sight in British trenches, which were mostly north of the French troops and seemed to be just where it always rained.

The troops lived in dug-outs—holes dug out of the sides of the trench. Sometimes the overhanging roof was supported with planks or sandbags to stop it falling in, and planks were then inserted to form a hard bed. Often two or three men slept above each other, as if on bunks. Blankets or groundsheets were hung from pegs in the trench wall to form a simple screen for privacy, but they offered no protection at all from shell splinters. It is difficult to imagine millions of men living like moles in earth trenches, sleeping on boards in holes scooped out of the mud; and yet these trenches were home for them all. There was no choice, and they soon got used to it.

Officers also lived in the trenches, but in better dug-outs deeper in the ground. Entry was normally past a sentry and down some steps to a small, cramped room, with planks for a roof and timber posts holding them up. Sometimes there were iron beds, probably found among the ruins of some village, and there was usually a table where maps could be unfolded by candlelight. Occasionally officers even managed to rig up an electric light, but shellfire usually broke the cables sooner or later.

German trenches and dug-outs were often more impressive than those of the British or French. Some of them had concrete defences, and most German dug-outs were deeper than British ones. Even ordinary German soldiers might live in a strong barrack-room 6 or 9 metres underground, safe from everything except a direct hit from a large shell. This feeling of greater safety was an important bonus for the Germans.

Trenches on both sides also had numerous home-made pieces of extra equipment. For example, gas was a common weapon in World War One, so many dug-outs had rubberised gas curtains hung up at the entrance as a simple protection for sleeping troops—though unfortunately they were not very effective. Most trenches also had a wind indicator, for a breeze was needed to blow gas towards the enemy. If the wind was blowing the wrong way, the troops were safe. Sentries also had a gas or attack warning signal, sometimes a hooter or just a gong made by hanging up an old shell case. At intervals along a trench there were also racks of distress rockets, to be used only when the men needed urgent help in battle. Considering they began as ditches where men took cover from gunfire, trenches quickly became very complicated.

Going up the line

For new arrivals straight from England, moving up to the front was a strange experience. As they approached the battle area the first hint of war was the rumble of distant artillery. Then as they drew closer they began to see the clear signs of war—enormous stock-piles of shells or tins of food, rows of heavy artillery under camouflage or among the trees, and narrow-gauge railways, part of the complicated supply system which fed and looked after the men in the front lines.

More ominous were the graveyards, with their rows of simple wooden crosses, and the hospitals. Any large building not yet badly damaged could be used as a hospital. Many churches, country houses, castles, schools and public halls had huge red crosses marked out on their roofs or lawns to identify them as hospitals.

Finally the new arrivals would reach the entrance to a communication trench and would begin to wind slowly in single file up to the front. Now the gunfire would be loud and shells might be seen exploding. Dead horses might lie by the track and the landscape would be torn and destroyed. By now most men would be feeling nervous.

Looking along a trench. One man stays on guard while others rest. The remains of a firing step can be seen with broken ammunition boxes lying nearby. The back wall of the trench has been strengthened with wood

Soon they would reach trenches with sinister names like Sniper's Alley or Dead Man's Corner painted up on signs, and it was time to keep their heads down. Some names, like Piccadilly or Sauchiehall Street, might remind them of home. Then they would reach the front line itself. The strongest impression was the smell—a sickening mixture of sweat, disinfectant, open latrines and the stench of rotting corpses.

Soon an officer would appear to take charge of the new arrivals. Private George Coppard, who later wrote a book about his life in the trenches, describes what happened next:

> He reminded us that we were on a war footing and that the severest military laws would apply for any dereliction of duty, such as desertion, mutiny, leaving the trenches without permiss-ion, cowardice, and sleeping while on sentry duty. A conviction by court martial for any such offence would carry the death sentence. The C.O. then directed the adjutant to read out the names of nearly a score of Tommies who had recently been sentenced to death by courts martial . . . I was stupified as the adjutant droned out each man's name, rank, unit and offence, followed in each case by the words 'and the sentence was duly carried out'. The hour and date of execution were also read out.

Then the troops would be shown their dug-outs and the planks they were to sleep on.

Daily life in the trenches

Most days were very monotonous, and seemed to pass very slowly. People were killed, but there were few great battles.

At first light the order 'Stand down' was given and the sentries could relax, knowing that the threat of a night raid by the enemy had passed. Then breakfast began and troops weary from peering into the dawn might get bacon, or at least a cup of tea brewed up on little fires all along the trenches, made from scraps of wood scavenged from local ruins.

Troops did not often go hungry, unless shelling interrupted the ferrying of supplies through the communication trenches, but the food was monotonous. There was always tinned 'bully beef' and usually a loaf of bread (which had to be shared among up to ten men). There was jam, but it always seemed to be Tickler's plum and apple variety and the men soon tired of it. Sometimes there was plenty of cheese, but it caused constipation. Some men believed this was deliberate, to ease the problem of trench lavatories. If nothing else was available, there were always emergency supplies of hard biscuits, but these were like cement and men with false teeth had to soak them in water.

Private George Coppard did not enjoy his food much:

> Wrapping loose rations such as tea, cheese and meat was not considered necessary, all being tipped into a sand-bag, a ghastly mix-up resulting. In wet weather their condition was unbelievable . . . Maconochie, a 'dinner in a tin', was my favourite and I could polish one off with gusto, but the usual share-out was one tin for four men.

Water was also a problem. Normally it was brought in petrol cans to the front, where chloride of lime was then added to kill off any germs—the taste was revolting. There was always a shortage of water, especially for washing and shaving, so troops sometimes collected rain water. In winter snow and ice were melted to make tea, but sometimes newly arrived men found bodies frozen in the ice as they broke off lumps to melt. It was a horrifying experience for the keen new troops.

By mid-morning, most troops were at work in the trenches, repairing damaged sections, filling sandbags, carrying supplies or running errands. Cleaning weapons was a common task: every man had a Lee Enfield rifle which had to be kept thoroughly clean in case it jammed at the vital moment.

Each day there was a medical check. Diseases were very common in the trenches, where men were crowded together in unhygienic conditions. Everyone had lice—in his hair, on his body and thriving in every fold of his clothing (Scottish kilts were especially bad). Occasionally men were de-loused behind the lines, but the lack of washing facilities meant that the lice reappeared after a few days of relief from itching. Rats also ran everywhere, feeding on rotting bodies and horse carcasses, and sometimes even nibbling the troops as they slept. It was not unusual to feel a rat run over your body as you lay in a dark dug-out.

'Trench foot' was a common complaint, caused by standing constantly in water. It started with the sort of wrinkles you get on your hands and feet from lying too long in a bath, but then it became worse, as Captain Edwin Venning noted:

> I have been talking to one of my stretcher-bearers. He has a foot swollen to three times its normal size: a great helpless bright pink lump. He has been stretcher-bearing over that awful ground almost the whole of four days. Changing his socks did no good . . . poor beggar! I shall be surprised if he doesn't lose that foot.

The troops were supposed to wash their feet regularly and rub them with whale oil, but it did little good. They were also supposed to change regularly into dry socks, but rain and mud made the new ones immediately wet again.

Much more serious, however, were the epidemics. Germs in food and water led to typhus, cholera and dysentery which killed thousands of men. Even measles and influenza raged through the crowded trenches.

For those who were wounded, there were no antibiotics. Wounds often went septic and led to gangrene. X-rays were rare, blood transfusions were not used in trenches and most needles were not sterilised. Many men died from infected wounds.

Much of the day was very boring. Most men just sat around reading or smoking or playing chess. Some wrote letters home. These were checked by a censor before being posted. Anything that might help the enemy was crossed out with a blue pencil—even a simple sentence like 'We are all feeling very tired after the recent fighting', for this might help the Germans to plan where or when to attack.

Every afternoon from two to four o'clock the Germans bombed and machine-gunned the trenches. This was called the 'afternoon strafe' and as long as you kept your head down you were generally safe. Even so, some explosives were lobbed over so as to land right in the trench, as Private George Coppard wrote:

Following a dull thud from close behind the enemy lines, we saw our first 'minnie', fired by a mortar-gun Jerry called *Minnenwerfer* [mine-thrower]. It was made from a steel drum packed with high explosives and scrap iron. When fired it sailed up into the air to 100 feet or so [about 30 metres] with a lighted fuse trailing from it, curving towards our lines. There was a couple of seconds to decide which way to run ... At last it descended hitting the ground with a smack ... The explosion was devastating, tearing one apart from concussion. Trenches were blasted into ruts. Men just disappeared and no one saw them go.

As long as the parapet was kept in good repair, bullets were less of a problem. Even so, ricochets did hit people with fearful suddenness—one moment you could be chatting with a pal, and the next he would drop dead 'like a

(left) *A letter sent from the front line. Study it carefully and notice how little information the troops were allowed to give. They could write longer letters when they were moved away from the front line.* (right) *A Christmas Card from the front line*

A remarkable photograph of a shell exploding only metres from a trench. Lumps of earth are being blasted in all directions. It is easy to imagine how a soldier could be torn to pieces in an explosion like this

puppet with the strings cut', as one soldier wrote. Snipers were another threat. Sometimes they would crawl out into No-Man's-Land at night. Even a lighted match could be fatal and soldiers never lit more than two cigarettes from one match before quickly putting it out. 'Never take the third light' was a common piece of advice.

For some men, the constant strain of living under shellfire, with splinters whizzing past and the din of explosions and gunfire ringing in their ears, led to a condition known as 'shell-shock'. The constant fear of being hit tore at their minds and reduced some men to nervous wrecks. From then on, any sudden noise might trigger their fear, causing them to take shelter or tremble and weep in terror. Early in the war, this mental illness was not recognised by the Army and many men were accused of cowardice, but later the problem was understood and shell-shock victims were sent home.

Eventually evening came to the trenches and the men settled down to sleep. Most of them would be disturbed by the cold, rats, explosions or false alarms. Few men slept for more than 3 or 4 hours. For the sentries, night was an anxious time of peering endlessly into the dark, trying to spot the enemy coming on a raid. The lives of everyone else depended on their vigilance. Any sentry found asleep was arrested and shot.

For some men, night meant work, perhaps a raid or an observation patrol into No-Man's-Land, trying to capture a prisoner or listen to the enemy talking. Others might have to repair the parapet or the barbed wire—dangerous work, for if the enemy heard their muffled hammering or whispering, star shells and flares would light the sky and machine-guns would sweep No-Man's-Land with a hail of bullets. Then eventually dawn arrived and the sentries stood down to begin another long day.

5 Trench Battles in France, 1914–1915

The idea of breakthrough

The early fighting in France was a war of movement as the Germans swept through France and Belgium. But then came the Battle of Ypres in October and November 1914. Here the Germans charged repeatedly in a frontal assault on the British troops and were mown down in a terrible slaughter. It should have been obvious after this that whichever side attacked would lose thousands of men. It was a stalemate—neither side could win if they did *not* attack but they would be slaughtered if they did.

On the other hand, the Germans were occupying French and Belgian territory. The Allies had to drive them out. This meant that the Germans could prepare strong defences

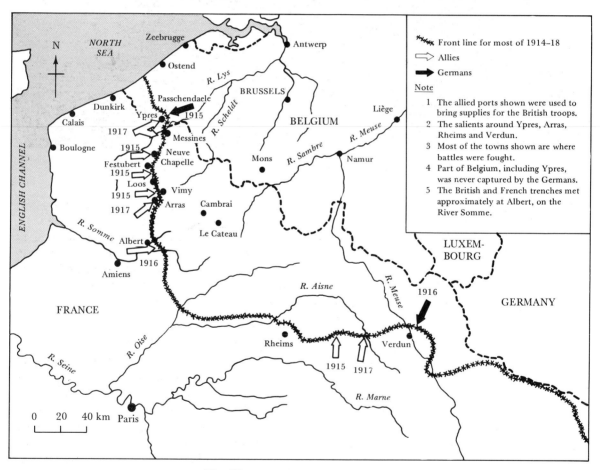

The Western Front, 1914–1918

A battlefield: dead trees, water-filled shell holes, duckboards and mud

and wait for the British or French to attack —and then massacre them with machine-gun fire. Faced with this problem, the Allied generals decided on a war of attrition. They *would* attack. They would lose thousands of men, but they would also kill many Germans. Eventually they would grind down the German Army until there was nothing left, even if only a handful of Allied troops also survived. It was a horrifying way to think, but fighting from trenches was a completely new kind of war. And so the rest of the war became a war of attrition and frontal assaults.

With trenches stretching from the coast of Belgium to Switzerland, there was no hope of manoeuvring round the enemy to attack from behind. The only chance was to collect a huge attacking force as secretly as possible and then batter right through the German trenches. With a hole punched through the enemy's defences, more troops could rush through to attack the Germans from behind, surrounding them, cutting them off from help, and finally defeating them. This was called a breakthrough.

Preparing for a battle

Every British attack was preceded by months of very careful planning. The most important thing was to select a good place to attack. On both sides some regiments were better fighters than others. Some had too many inexperienced recruits, or had suffered heavy casualties, or had too many old men, for example. As a result, both sides constantly raided each other at night

The effects of an artillery bombardment: dead Germans in the remains of their dug-out. The black specks on the corpses are bluebottles

to find out which regiments occupied the trenches opposite. From prisoners taken on these raids, interrogators learned what sort of troops waited across No-Man's-Land. At headquarters their reports built up a picture of the other side's strengths and weaknesses, from which the place of attack was selected.

The next step was to prepare the men. Some were sent on leave for a rest. Others were marched to secret locations for training, and then on to reserve trenches in the selected battle area. Slowly thousands of men began to gather, often billeted in villages or even ruins in an effort to deceive enemy pilots. It was difficult to disguise the presence of such huge numbers and by now the enemy would probably have

guessed from the huge piles of supplies and shells, even if the men remained hidden.

A few days before the battle was due to begin, the artillery started to bombard the enemy trenches. The communication trenches were blasted to prevent reinforcements reaching the front lines. The front lines were also shelled to kill the defenders and destroy the barbed wire. This terrifying bombardment might go on, night and day, for up to a week, giving the Germans no time to relax or prepare.

The Germans soon learned that an artillery bombardment meant a coming battle, and trains and lorries rushed thousands of men to the danger zone. By the time the attack began the temporary superiority of numbers secretly built up behind the British lines was matched by reinforcements on the German side.

During the night before the attack, British troops crept out into No-Man's-Land to cut their barbed wire. This allowed the men through for the attack. Officers synchronised watches and the troops moved up towards the front line, crowding into every trench. At dawn the shelling suddenly stopped. There was a moment's silence. Then officers blew whistles and, placing short ladders against the parapet, the men went 'over the top'. The first men pulled back the barbed wire as the others set off into No-Man's-Land.

Some slithered back dead before they could even clamber out of their trench. Many more fell in the charge as the German machine-guns opened up. Wounded men writhed about

screaming in agony but death came very suddenly, as one soldier described:

> You could always tell when a man was shot dead. A wounded man always tried to break his own fall. A dead man generally fell forward, his balance tending in that direction, and he bent simultaneously at the knees, waist, neck and ankles.

Meanwhile hospitals dealt with the returning flood of wounded men. Field dressing stations just behind the front lines patched up small wounds. Mobile field hospitals handled more serious cases, and really badly injured men were sent to base hospitals for more complicated treatment. From there, some were sent to Britain, or 'Blighty', as the troops called home. Many men envied those who 'copped a

Going over the top. Canadian troops clamber over a trench parapet at the start of the attack. The man in front and the man nearest the camera have almost certainly been hit already

Blighty'. Later in the war, some deliberately shot themselves, perhaps through the foot or hand, hoping that this would make them unfit for further duty and that they would be sent home. If it was proved that their wounds were self-inflicted, they were executed.

The infantryman

In the First World War foot soldiers or infantrymen were supposed to attack quickly through gaps in the enemy's defences. In reality this was impossible, especially on the Allied side, because of the barbed wire, the mud, and the heavy pack each man carried. Indeed, as the war went on this pack actually grew heavier. In August 1914 it weighed 59lb 11oz (27kg), but by Christmas alone this had risen to 66lb (30kg). Apart from weapons, soldiers had to carry into an attack a shovel, wire-cutters, sandbags, a gas-mask, 170 bullets (surprisingly heavy), plus personal clothing and 'iron rations' consisting of 1lb (½kg) corned beef, tea, sugar, and two packs of hard biscuits. In an attack the infantryman was supposed to live for days on his iron rations, washed down with whatever tea he could brew in his mess-tin over some solidified paraffin (which always flavoured the tea anyway). By 1915 most troops also had steel helmets, which were very heavy and often caused headaches. Finally every man carried cooking and washing equipment and in winter thigh-length rubber boots and a leather jerkin.

The battles of 1915

The first battle was a French attack in January in the open countryside of Champagne, east of

Field ambulances waiting for wounded men during an attack. One cart carries collapsible stretchers and there are more on the ground nearby

44

Two men with the heavy packs they had to carry into battle. The soldier on the left shows his back pack and steel helmet, gas-mask, haversack, ammunition pouches and water-bottle. The man on the right shows, in addition, his cooking dixie, a bag of hand grenades and bayonet. Both men carry a Lee Enfield rifle

Rheims. The BEF was small, so the French did most of the fighting. The French troops charged with great spirit and determination but were stopped by machine-guns. Well over 100,000 French soldiers died or were wounded for a gain of no more than 8 kilometres. Eventually the attacks ended in March with no breakthrough.

In March the British launched an attack at Neuve Chapelle. This was the first offensive by British troops in France and they wanted to do well. The Germans did not regard the small BEF as a threat and most enemy troops were to the south facing the French. As a result the British actually broke right through the German lines, but then everything stopped at the moment of success. Officers hesitated to keep going, orders did not get through, field telephones did not work, and during the first night this gave the Germans time to move a few machine-guns into position. Next day, it is said that only twelve German machine-guns stopped the entire British Army advancing any further. There were no shells left to destroy these machine-guns, and the whole attack ground to a halt. There were 13,000 British dead or wounded—nothing like the losses in later battles, but the British public was shocked. One ruined village was captured, but the Germans realised that the French were no longer the only threat. Now every future British attack would be much more difficult.

In April the Germans attacked at Ypres, where they had lost heavily in 1914. They were still hoping to end the war quickly in France and concentrate fully on defeating Russia. The 'Second Battle of Ypres' is best remembered as the first attack in which poison gas was used in France (page 57). The gas caused great panic but did not create a breakthrough for the Germans. The British, Canadians and French defended grimly and then counter-attacked, until eventually both sides gave up, exhausted. Now battle casualties were rising: the British lost 60,000 and the Germans 35,000. They were losses which the small BEF in particular could not afford.

In May the French attacked in the Artois area at Vimy Ridge. Once again the French charged fearlessly into devastating machine-gun fire, right to the crest of the hill, but they lost 100,000 men and never made the top. Two years later the Canadians attacked up the same slopes (page 52) and found the skeletons and ragged uniforms of thousands of Frenchmen still lying on the battlefield.

In May the British attacked Aubers Ridge. As the troops advanced they were mown down in rows by German machine-gunners—the slow, heavily laden troops were an easy target as they stumbled shoulder-to-shoulder towards the defenders. The attack was a complete failure. There were not even enough shells to kill the machine-gunners. This angered the British public and led to much criticism of the Liberal government.

Meanwhile the British also attacked nearby at Festubert. Here they pushed the Germans back 800 metres for the loss of 27,000 more men. Once again there were not enough artillery shells, so there was no breakthrough.

In September the French attacked again in Champagne. They drove the Germans back little more than 3 kilometres and lost 100,000 men. The cavalry, waiting to charge through the expected gap in the German lines, was never used, and there was no breakthrough. The French also tried again at Vimy, but again they did not capture the ridge and they simply threw away another 50,000 lives.

Finally the British attacked at Loos, among the pit-heads and coal tips of this mining town. Once more the frontal attacks made no progress against the machine-guns. Twenty Scottish regiments took part in this battle—the greatest number ever to fight together in a British army—but even their spirit and the skirling of the bagpipes were of little use against barbed wire and machine-guns. For months after, the red kilts of the Camerons and the dark colours of the Black Watch and Gordon Highlanders could be seen caught on the barbed wire among the more anonymous khaki uniforms of the English troops. During this battle German troops called the kilted Scots the 'Ladies from Hell'—a nickname which they kept long after. It was a costly end to the fighting of 1915. When the year finally ended, victory was no closer to either side. The search for a breakthrough had failed.

6 Slaughter in France, 1916–1917

Lord Kitchener's Army

The British Expeditionary Force which sailed to France in 1914 was a peacetime army—very experienced, well trained, but too small to fight by itself. It had to be helped by a new army of volunteers. Recruiting these men was one of the first tasks taken on by the government when war was declared on 4 August.

On 6 August the government asked Lord Kitchener to organise the recruiting campaign. He was a famous army general, well known to the public because of his successful campaigns in past African wars, and it was hoped that his popularity would encourage people to join the Army. Soon Lord Kitchener's face and pointing finger appeared on posters all over Britain, urging young men to enlist.

Kitchener hoped for 100,000 volunteers in six months, but he underestimated the tremendous feelings of patriotism and enthusiasm which were sweeping Britain at that moment. The response to his call was fantastic: 500,000 men joined up in August alone. An average of 180,000 enlisted each month after that until by January 1916, about 3½ million men had volunteered.

Recruiting offices all over Britain were swamped with crowds of men eager to 'take the King's shilling' (their first day's pay). Thousands were turned away each day because recruiting stations simply could not cope with such huge numbers. Many factories and offices lost half their men overnight as workers decided, often just on impulse, to join up and 'do their duty'. Many senior school pupils enlisted, and some boys who were under age volunteered by giving false ages.

The government encouraged men to enlist in various ways. Regiments such as the Artists' Rifles were created for people from similar

A recruiting poster from 1915. Thousands of men responded to Lord Kitchener's pointing finger. Study the small print at the bottom which gives rates of pay. The flags represent the Allies. Left to right: France, Russia, Britain, Belgium, Japan

backgrounds. In the industrial cities of the north of England many 'Pals' Battalions' were formed so that men from one town could all fight and live in the trenches together—sadly they also died together. Of the thousand men who formed a Pals' Battalion in the small Lancashire town of Accrington, 234 were killed on

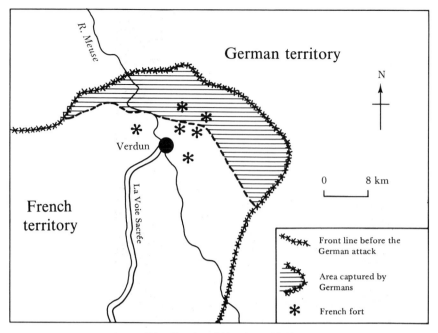

The Battle of Verdun, 1916

the same day and another 350 were wounded.

So many men volunteered in the early weeks of the war that it was impossible to provide them all with uniforms or weapons or even proper army barracks. Many men marched with walking sticks instead of rifles to begin with, but despite these problems their training went on through the winter and into 1915. By the end of 1915 they formed 'Kitchener's New Armies', ready to sail for France to replace the BEF's casualties.

The arrival of these fit and keen young men led to the planning of a new campaign for the spring of 1916. It was decided to combine with the French for a huge attack in the valley of the River Somme. Despite the heavy losses they had suffered in many useless attacks during 1915, the Allies still believed that this time, with fresh troops and new enthusiasm, they would defeat the Germans simply by attacking with overwhelming numbers. This was to prove a disastrous belief.

Planning for this great battle went on during early 1916 but then everything was upset when the Germans unexpectedly attacked the French at Verdun.

The Battle of Verdun, 1916

Verdun was a carefully chosen target. It stood on the River Meuse in a salient (bulge) in the French trenches which pushed out into German-held territory. Normally it was unwise to hold a salient because the enemy could fire into the trenches from at least three sides, but Verdun was special to the French. It was the greatest symbol of defiance against the Germans, a city the Germans had never captured, even during their first invasion in 1914. Now the French were determined not to give it up. As if to emphasise this determination, Verdun was protected by a number of strong underground concrete forts.

Perhaps it seems surprising that the Germans chose to attack the very city the French were most determined to defend, but in fact this is exactly what the Germans wanted. The city was like a huge trap. The Germans needed only to attack with a fairly small army and the French would respond by pulling men away from other areas and packing them into the Verdun salient—where they would be slaughtered by shellfire and gas. The Germans would

French troops in a trench at Verdun. Their blue-grey helmets and uniforms were different from those of British troops

'bleed the French white' and the spirit of the French Army would collapse.

The German attacks began on 21 February 1916 and took the French completely by surprise. First came a nine-hour bombardment by 1,200 field guns, about one for every 12 metres of the 13-kilometre front line, and then the shell-shocked survivors were attacked by crack German assault troops. For three days the French held out in the remains of their flimsy trenches under a rain of shellfire and gas, but on the fourth day the outer defences of Verdun were finally overrun.

A new commander was sent to the city, General Pétain. An expert on defensive fighting, he was much respected by ordinary French soldiers because he had fought among the men at the River Marne in 1914 while other generals were issuing orders from the safety of remote headquarters. His first message to the weary defenders was 'Hold fast, I have confidence in you'—and they responded. But it was a difficult task, and thousands of men were killed or maimed by the constant artillery fire as every metre was bitterly fought for. Trenches just disappeared into heaps of earth and countless

49

men were buried alive. Corpses rotted with a foul stench as warmer weather came. And each day the Germans crept forward a little more. Every so often the French made desperate counter-attacks and were cut to ribbons by machine-gun fire, sacrificing themselves to save Verdun.

Only one road into the town remained open. It soon earned the nickname *La Voie Sacrée*, The Sacred Way, for everything needed by the hard-pressed defenders had to be carried along it. Night and day, lorries streamed in each direction along this one road, ferrying men, ammunition, food and medicines into the battle area, and bringing out an endless procession of wounded. About 12,000 vehicles were used to keep the supplies moving.

As spring turned into summer, the French defenders were still desperately hanging on. Then the tide turned. The British attacked in the Somme area and General Brusilov led a huge Russian attack against the Austrians. The Germans, who had themselves lost vast numbers of men at Verdun, were forced to give up and send troops to deal with these British and Russian attacks.

Verdun was the first really horrifying battle of World War One. Thousands of men never recovered from the awful sights they had seen. 'We eat, we drink beside the dead, we sleep in the midst of the dying, we laugh and sing in the company of corpses,' wrote a French soldier. It is estimated that about 300,000 Germans were killed and about 350,000 French. Over 23 million shells were fired by the two sides—over 150,000 every single day, exploding into shrapnel, maiming, blinding and killing. General Pétain was now a French hero, but his famous words *'Ils ne passeront pas!'* ('They shall not pass!') were bought with a terrible sacrifice.

The Battle of the Somme, 1916

While the fighting raged at Verdun the British made new plans for the attack in the valley of the River Somme. Obviously the French would not be able to take part as originally intended, and in fact only five French divisions attacked on the first day, compared with fourteen British divisions. This was the first important battle where the British provided a larger proportion of the troops than the French.

The attack was supposed to be planned in great secrecy, but long before it started the Germans knew all about it. Their spotter planes watched the complicated preparations, their tunnellers overheard British messages as signallers shouted into field telephones, and all that remained was to discover exactly *when* the attack would come. Meanwhile the German barbed wire was strengthened and dug-outs were made even deeper. German troops practised carrying their heavy machine-guns up from their dug-outs until they could do it in 3 minutes, which would give plenty of time between the end of the preliminary bombardment and the arrival of the first British troops. During the last week of June the bombardment began, and went on for days. Then German signallers intercepted a 'good luck' message from General Rawlinson, commander for the coming attack, and any last chance of a surprise was gone. Five hours later the bombardment stopped and the battle began.

The first men went 'over the top' at 7.30 am on 1 July 1916. It was a beautiful sunny morning and in the lull between the bombardment and the start of machine-gun fire the soldiers could hear birds singing. As untried civilian volunteers, they were trained simply to clamber over the trench parapet and form 'waves' of about 1,000 men, two paces between each man, and then advance at walking pace towards the Germans. More waves would follow at 90-metre intervals. They were told that the Germans and their trenches would have been blasted by the preliminary bombardment and that the wire would have been destroyed.

In fact they went straight into the worst slaughter ever suffered by a British army. The wire was not even damaged—explosions had merely sent it flying up into the air, to come back down intact. Thousands of men died trying to struggle through it. The deep bunkers had not been destroyed either, and from them the Germans slaughtered the British waves as they advanced across the open ground of No-Man's-Land. About 20,000 British were

An artillery battery firing during the Battle of the Somme. These guns are 8-inch howitzers of the 39th Siege Battery of the Royal Garrison Artillery

killed that day, and 40,000 were wounded. Even at Verdun the worst French losses for a whole month were not as bad as the British losses on that one day.

The battle went on for another five months but it was already lost. Here and there the Germans were pushed back a little, but there was no breakthrough. When troops did occasionally burst through the front line, poor leadership gave the Germans time to defend the second line. The cavalry were too far away to take advantage of any gains. A night attack was tried, but that also failed. In desperation General Rawlinson even used a few tanks; these had only recently been invented, but there were not enough of them to win the battle and it only gave away knowledge of this secret weapon. Bad weather finally brought the battle to an

end in November. By then the British had lost a staggering 419,654 men and the French another 204,253. The Germans had lost about 600,000 men but their front line was still intact. There had been over a million casualties in a battle which did not bring victory any closer to either side.

The Nivelle Offensive, 1917

Winter brought another temporary halt to the slaughter but the planners were already preparing for another spring offensive in 1917. Because there was still no sign of victory, General Joffre, commander-in-chief of the French armies, was replaced by General Nivelle, who arrived with the confident words 'I have the formula!'. He immediately began planning a

51

new attack in the valley of the River Aisne. Following heavy losses at Verdun and the Somme, the morale of the French troops was very low. But Nivelle brilliantly convinced his men that this battle would definitely bring victory, and when the attack began in April 1917 they were once again confident and keen.

The offensive was a complete failure. There was no secrecy. The weather was bad, and the confident French troops were mown down by sweeping machine-gun fire as they clambered uphill against uncut barbed wire. Nivelle's troops captured a few kilometres of shell-torn battlefield, but they lost over 200,000 men and there was no breakthrough. The high spirits and false hopes of the French armies collapsed. They refused to fight any more.

The French Army mutinies

For about six weeks in 1917, from the end of April to June, many French troops simply refused to obey orders. They had suffered enough, and even loyal regiments with excellent fighting records now rebelled. Troops on leave rioted at railway stations and would not return to the fighting area. Some troops demonstrated with red flags, inspired by the Russian Revolution which had taken place in March (see Chapter 12). Others threatened to march on Paris, perhaps to overthrow the government and make peace with Germany. In many places French trenches were completely undefended as soldiers deserted rather than go into another battle just to be slaughtered. Anti-war leaflets were passed among many regiments and at one time troops of fifty-four divisions were 'on strike'. It was an extremely serious situation for the French government.

General Nivelle was sacked and replaced by General Pétain, the hero of Verdun. He saved the day. In the first month he visited troops in over ninety divisions, listening to their grievances about pay, conditions, leave and the pointless losses in battle. Then he promised that if the troops would return to their trenches to *defend* France, he would not waste them on any more costly attacks. At the same time, fifty-five ringleaders were executed, and many

more were given long prison sentences. This combination of sternness and sympathy for the troops worked, and the men returned to their trenches. The danger was over.

Surprisingly the Germans never learned about the mutiny. If they had they could have won the war in 1917, for Paris was only 104 kilometres from the front line, and at one point only two loyal division stood in the way. But the Germans did not believe their spies until it was too late.

The fighting at Vimy Ridge, 1917

The Nivelle Offensive was yet another disaster. Part of the plan, however, involved a British attack to the north, where it was hoped they would divert enough Germans to give Nivelle a better chance with the main attack. This British battle was a success.

By 1917 the British had learned from their failure at the Somme. Artillery fire was now much more accurate. The infantry were more experienced. Shells were more plentiful and plans were better prepared.

It was decided to attack the German-held hill at Vimy Ridge, near the town of Arras. You will remember that French troops had failed to capture this hill in 1915 (page 46). Thousands of troops were hidden in cellars and caves all over the town, and special tunnels were dug to allow these men to move up to the front line without being spotted. On 4 April the preliminary bombardment began from nearly a thousand field guns. Then on 9 April the troops, mostly Canadians, went 'over the top' in heavy sleet and snow after a bombardment which had used up over a million shells in just five days. Even then the shelling continued in a new tactic known as a 'creeping barrage'.

This meant that the artillery gradually increased their distance as the soldiers advanced. It required great skill to avoid hitting your own men or shelling too far in front of them as they moved forward. Ideally the shells were supposed to land about 200 metres in front of the advancing infantry. This time the tactic worked excellently and shells were still falling as the Canadians attacked.

The advance had begun at 5.30 am, and by midday the British and empire troops were standing on top of the ridge looking over the unspoiled countryside beyond. The Germans counter-attacked but they were too late. The British hesitated to take advantage of this breakthrough, however, and when they finally moved on they were also too late. At Bullecourt, for example, the Australians were massacred by German soldiers hidden in hastily prepared new defences. Nevertheless the success at Vimy Ridge was very welcome after years of defeats, and today the memorial to all Canadians killed in France stands on the crest of the ridge.

The Third Battle of Ypres, 1917

Like Verdun, Ypres (or 'Wipers' as the British troops called it) stood in a dangerous salient which the Germans could fire into from three sides. There had already been battles there in 1914 and 1915 and now it was to become a battlefield yet again.

The commander-in-chief of the British armies, General Haig, decided to break out of this salient in a daring push towards the Belgian coast. He believed the Germans were exhausted after so many tough battles, and he wanted to capture the Belgian ports of Zeebrugge and Ostende. These were important bases for German submarines, which were sinking an alarming number of British ships in 1917. In addition the mutinies among the French troops (mentioned earlier in this chapter) began at this moment and an attack would help distract the Germans. So there was great pressure to succeed in the attack at Ypres. In fact there were a number of separate battles in different parts of the salient.

The attack at Messines Ridge, 1917

To begin with all went very well. For a year miners had been digging twenty-two tunnels under Messines Ridge, a German-held hill which overlooked many British trenches around Ypres. It was dark and dangerous work, for the Germans were always listening for

(left to right) *General Haig (commander of the British troops), General Joffre (commander of the French troops) and Lloyd George*

the sounds of tunnelling and would sometimes dig their own underground passages, trying to find the miners. When the two sides met there were ferocious underground battles with picks and shovels. Sometimes men were buried alive as the tunnels collapsed, but the work still went on. Eventually all the tunnels, varying from 35 to 350 metres long, were estimated to be directly under the German front-line trenches, and they were packed with dynamite. At 3.10 am on 7 June 1917 a million pounds of high explosive blew up right under the feet of the Germans.

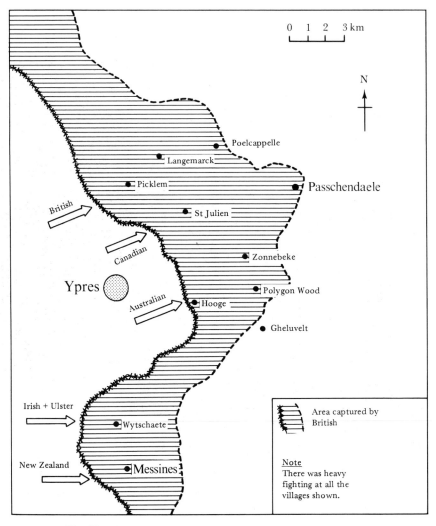

The Third Battle of Ypres: Messines and Passchendaele

The effect was shattering. Nineteen of the tunnels exploded with a noise that could be heard in London, 208 kilometres away. The night was lit up by a red glow as sheets of flame shot up through the ground, which shook like an earthquake. About 10,000 Germans were killed instantly, buried alive by falling earth, or thrown high into the air like rag dolls. British field guns immediately began firing and 80,000 British, Irish, Australian and New Zealand troops charged at the bewildered German survivors. By midday the entire ridge was captured. The Germans lost over 25,000 men, and

another 7,500 were captured, but even in this victory the British lost 17,000.

Passchendaele, 1917

Messines Ridge lay south of Ypres, but the main attack was to the north, on the flat land of Flanders. Now everything started to go wrong. The weather turned very wet and the battle area became virtually flooded. Also, any chance of taking the Germans by surprise was lost for the main attack did not begin until 31 July—a fatal delay of six weeks after Messines

A sergeant of the Lancashire Fusiliers climbs out of his flooded dug-out in a front-line trench near Ypres. Notice the barbed wire in the background

Ridge, which gave the Germans plenty of time to strengthen their defences.

As at Vimy Ridge in April, the troops moved forward behind a creeping barrage from the artillery. But there was one important difference. The ground here was flat, and soggy from the recent rain. The whole battlefield soon turned into a sea of mud, making it impossible for horses, tanks, guns or supplies to advance. Even the soldiers could hardly move through the porridge-like slime, which often reached their knees. Normally it took only two men to carry a stretcher, but now sixteen were needed, stumbling through the dreadful mud. Wounded men fell into the mire and simply sank out of sight. Horses and guns disappeared

without trace in a landscape of water-filled shell holes, tree stumps and endless mud.

It was hopeless to attack in such conditions but General Haig insisted that the British should keep struggling on. They lost 30,000 men in the first week. The figure reached 67,000 by the end of the first month, by which time only about 5 kilometres of devastated swampland had been won. For the first time since the start of the war, the spirits of the British troops fell sharply. It all seemed so futile.

By October the fighting had reached the ruins of what had once been the village of Passchendaele, about 11 kilometres from the British starting point. Any hope of breaking

Mud at Ypres. A horse and water-cart have slipped off the brushwood track across a muddy area. Problems like this were common during the rainy Battle of Ypres. In the end the mud made fighting impossible

through to the Belgian coast had now been abandoned, for the rain was still coming down in torrents. 'The ground is like a bog,' wrote General Haig, the British commander-in-chief. 'The mud is our most effective ally,' wrote a German commander. On 6 November the Canadians finally captured Passchendaele, for what it was worth, and six days later the fighting died down. The British had lost about 250,000 men. The Germans had lost about 200,000. It was a dreadful price to pay for 11 kilometres of mud.

7 Tanks and Gas

We have seen how battles in France usually turned into slaughter. Attacks were always halted by machine-gun fire or shrapnel from artillery fire. And yet year after year the generals on both sides still sent their troops into battle in the same way. Not surprisingly the casualty figures multiplied each year. The blowing up of Messines Ridge in 1917 was about the only battle where anything different was tried. Even night attacks and smoke screens were little used.

Unfortunately, many of the senior generals had very out-of-date ideas. There *were* new weapons—machine-guns, aeroplanes, submarines—but they were often ignored. Lord Kitchener, for example, said that four machine-guns per battalion would be enough and any more would be an unnecessary luxury. Meanwhile the Germans had sixteen per battalion, and by the end of the war even the British had forty per battalion.

The generals still believed that cavalry would win wars, as they had often done before the invention of the machine-gun. General Haig even said that 'cavalry will have a larger sphere of action in future wars'. This now seems a very silly thing to say but in 1914 most commanders agreed with him. France, Germany, Austria and Russia each had over 100,000 cavalry, which they believed would be vital for winning battles. In fact they were hardly ever used, especially in the mud and barbed wire of France.

Nevertheless, as the slaughter continued and the public at home demanded to know why victory was not yet in sight, the generals were forced to consider some of the new military inventions. One example was the flame-thrower. Could it bring victory where frontal assaults had failed?

The flamethrower consisted of a can of petrol which a soldier carried on his back, connected to a hose through which he squirted the liquid towards the enemy. The hose had a trigger and a sparking mechanism, so when the soldier fired, the petrol was set on fire and a stream of burning liquid sailed through the air at the enemy. A skilful operator could make his flame land with some accuracy on a hidden target, like a machine-gun post. He could even direct the flame through the narrow slit windows of concrete forts and kill or burn the defenders inside. The Germans used this weapon quite a lot, especially at Verdun where it caused great panic among the French. But it did not help to shorten the war or even win battles. In fact it was quite likely to explode and kill the soldier using it.

Gas warfare

A more common weapon was gas. This was first used by the Germans in Russia in 1915 but it was soon adopted by all the armies. The first that British or French troops knew of it was at Ypres in April 1915. It appeared as a greenish-yellow cloud which gradually changed into a bluish-white mist, drifting with the wind towards the Allied trenches. Here it created utter terror—no one knew what to do. It is said that some young officers, remembering their simple schoolboy science, advised their men to urinate into their handkerchiefs and hold them to their noses as a primitive disinfectant. Not surprisingly it did not work.

Soon gas-masks were distributed to the troops on both sides. The wearer breathed in through a tin filled with chemicals, which acted as a filter against the gas. This tin of chemicals

A German flamethrower in action. These Germans are practising against a captured British tank

could be changed when it was used up, or if a new form of gas appeared. The German gas-mask had the filter in a drum in front of the mouth, which forced the wearer to breathe both in and out through it, making it stuffy and awkward to fight in. It was also uncomfortable to wear, being made of heavily oiled leather. The British gas-mask, which was better, had the filter in a haversack which the soldier wore on his chest, and which was linked to his mouth by a tube. The mask itself was usually made of canvas, with shatter-proof eye pieces, and a valve which allowed the wearer to breathe out normally, which was more comfortable. There were even gas-masks for horses.

To begin with, gases were mostly lung irritants such as chlorine or phosgene. They were released from cylinders when the wind was blowing in the right direction and allowed to drift towards the enemy. Later, gas shells were introduced, and Wilfred Owen's poem 'Dulce et Decorum Est', which you may know, describes such an attack. The idea of these lung irritants was to make defenders gasp for air while the other side attacked. Later, 'tear producers' were introduced. These caused such irritation and watering of the eyes that the defenders could not fight back when the enemy arrived. Other gases attacked the nervous system or caused various degrees of paralysis, and these were more lethal. Then in 1917 there appeared 'mustard gas', the most notorious of all. This was like an acid. It burnt the skin and caused blisters, but it also formed a foam in the lungs which could be fatal. The normal British gas-mask gave no protection against it and it was greatly feared by the Allied troops, for it was also colourless and had no smell. The

Allies used gas too, but not on the same scale as the Germans.

Strangely enough, for all the terror it caused, gas did not kill as many men as might have been expected. About ninety thousand soldiers altogether were killed by gas, and well over a million men were injured or blinded by it. In France, the British lost about 6,000 men, and another 180,000 were injured or blinded. Most of these were mustard-gas casualties. Russia suffered most of all—about 56,000 of those killed by gas were Russians, few of whom had gas-masks.

In the end the use of gas was unsuccessful, for two main reasons. The wind in France generally blew towards the Germans, which prevented them from using it very often. Also, as the war went on, the Germans began to run out of chemicals, with the result that they never had enough gas at any one time to win a battle.

The development of the tank

One weapon which probably did help to bring victory was the tank. The idea was not new but it had never been taken seriously by army experts. When early plans for a tank were offered to the government by a Nottingham plumber, for example, the papers were simply put aside with 'The man's mad' written across them. Later, when a tank was actually demonstrated to Lord Kitchener in 1916, his only comment was, 'A pretty mechanical toy, but the war will never be won by such machines.'

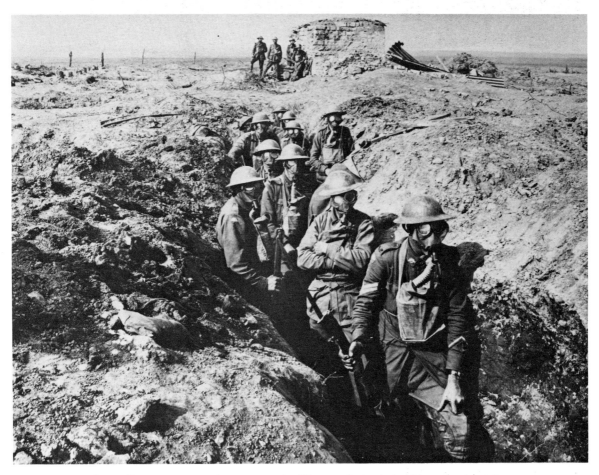

Australian troops wearing gas-masks. The respirator is kept in a chest haversack and is connected to the face-mask by a tube

A typical British tank

The tank was based on the prewar caterpillar tractor, widely used on muddy farms. When a Colonel Swinton suggested adding a few guns and some armour plating round it, the idea was rejected by the Army but taken up by the Admiralty under Winston Churchill. The Navy spent £75,000 on improving the design, and early tanks were even called 'land ships' in an attempt to explain why the Navy was involved.

Eventually the government gave in. So long as the machine could travel at 4 mph (6 kph), turn sharply, reverse, climb a 1-in-1 slope of at least 5 feet (1½ metres), cross a gap of 8 feet (2½ metres), keep going for at least 20 miles (32 kilometres) and carry a crew of ten plus two machine-guns and a cannon, they would agree to it. Soon the first prototype appeared, nicknamed 'Big Willie' after the German Kaiser. It was so successful in trials over the worst possible hilly and muddy ground that it was accepted and more were built. When the first of these new weapons were sent to France, they were unloaded from ships covered in tarpaulins and labelled 'Water Tanks' to mislead German spies. The name 'tank' has stuck to them ever since.

Life in a tank

Most early tanks carried a crew of about eight men, crowded into the small space round the huge engine. Conditions inside were terrible. The engine gave off strong fumes and became so hot that crewmen wore leather jerkins over their uniforms, to protect them when they were thrown against the hot moving parts as the tank lurched across the battlefield. The temperature inside a tank could reach over 38°C, which quickly exhausted the cramped and sweating crewmen. In addition the noise was so loud that the commander's orders had to be given by hand signal. And all the time bullets might be ricocheting off the sides of the tank as it scraped over barbed wire or bumped over shell holes and trenches. Inside, the men were thrown about as they fed ammunition to the machine-gunners, and the gearsman or driver concentrated on keeping formation with other tanks.

Quite often tanks broke down in battle. Sometimes the caterpillar tracks came off, or the engine stopped. Often tanks ran out of petrol and some were damaged by artillery fire, but whatever the reason it spelled great danger for the crew inside. While the tank was moving they were fairly safe, but now they were an easy target as they clambered out through the hatches.

The Battle of Cambrai, 1917

As we saw in the last chapter (page 51), the secret of the tank was given away during the Battle of the Somme in 1916 in a desperate attempt to snatch victory when the infantry were being slaughtered. It came as a complete surprise to the Germans. Their front-line troops were terrified by the seemingly unstoppable monsters—but there were not nearly enough of them to help win the battle. Surprisingly the Germans did not take tanks seriously, believing them to be just another short-lived idea, and they did not do much to develop their own tanks.

Although Allied tanks were used in several more battles, they are best remembered for their attack at Cambrai in November 1917. This town was part of the Hindenburg Line, a well-prepared series of deep concrete forts, with well-fortified trenches, thick barbed wire and even a wide anti-tank ditch—a place where the Germans certainly did not expect an attack. But the ground here was firm and not too churned up by shellfire—just the place where tanks could prove their worth and help the

A tank smashes through barbed wire

infantry burst a hole through the enemy trenches. It was decided to attack here, and a secret operation began as the Army collected as many tanks as possible for a great charge through the enemy lines.

At 6.20 am on 20 November, about 1,000 field guns suddenly started pounding the German trenches, and immediately 378 tanks, supported by 289 aircraft, started lumbering forward 'looking like giant toads', as one soldier said. Many tanks carried 'fascines'—huge rolls of tightly bundled brushwood—and these were thrown down into the anti-tank ditch to fill it up and give the tanks something to drive over. It was the first time that such large numbers of tanks had ever been used. They easily crushed the barbed wire and smashed through the German trenches. By 4 o'clock the British tanks had punched a hole 10 kilometres wide and 6 kilometres deep through the German lines. It was a great moment for the tank leader, Major-General Elles, whose own tank even flew a huge flag as he charged into battle.

Unfortunately everything now started to go wrong. There were not enough infantry to take advantage of this huge hole in the German defences, and the enemy soon began to recover and fight back. By evening many tanks had broken down—over a hundred from lack of petrol or engine failure and another sixty-five from enemy gunfire, including sixteen knocked out by a single German field gun. All these tanks were now stranded in German territory, and there were no reserves. The surviving crews were exhausted after a very long day's battle and they could do nothing to help as the cavalry, sent in to take advantage of the break-through, were cut to pieces by a few machine-guns. In the following days the British infantry were gradually pushed back again and the war returned to its normal course of slaughter.

Nevertheless, tanks had shown that they could batter through enemy defences where troops on foot or on horseback could not. Now they were used wherever the ground was suitable.

8 Russia and Turkey

So far, the story of World War One has concentrated on France and the 'Western Front'. But if you think back to how the war began (pages 21-22) you will realise that fighting was going on elsewhere too—this is why it was called a *world* war. Some battles were in other parts of Europe, but campaigns were also fought far away from Europe.

In Africa the British used Nigerian, Rhodesian, South African and other colonial troops to capture German territories. Some fell easily, but German East Africa (Tanganyika, now Tanzania) was very large and two rival armies, both assisted by native trackers, hunted each other right to the end of the war. British gunboats were even dragged through the jungle to Lake Tanganyika to operate against the Germans.

In Asia the Japanese, allies of Britain, attacked the German trading colony at Kiaochow in China. The Japanese did very little else during the war, but this attack did at least deny the German Navy the use of an important harbour.

Africa and Asia are two examples of the war being fought in other distant parts of the world, but there were also more important fighting areas.

The Eastern Front

When Russia went to war on 1 August 1914 the Germans confidently expected that it would be at least six weeks before any Russian troops would be ready to attack. Russia, however, astonished the world by sending *two* armies into Germany in just ten days. This helped to disrupt the Schlieffen Plan and to save France by forcing the Germans to send extra troops to the 'Eastern Front'.

The Russian armies have been described as being like a steamroller—huge and unstoppable once they got going. However, they were led by lazy, incompetent officers. The troops were mostly tough, uncomplaining peasant farm labourers, but they lacked equipment. Some had no boots or winter coats. Sometimes two or three men shared one rifle. Usually they were short of bullets, and they always needed more medical supplies. Artillery units were badly organised, never had enough shells, had old-fashioned guns and hopeless officers. The cavalry still rode with sabres and lances. The army may have been enormous, but it was sadly out of date.

In addition, Russia was a very backward country. There were not enough steelworks, explosives factories, railways, hospitals, shipyards, companies making medicines, and so on. Supplies got bogged down on dreadful roads. Military commands got lost on a dilapidated, rickety telegraph system. In short, the Russian effort on the Eastern Front was a shambles.

To start with, in 1914, all seemed to go well. Russian troops easily pushed 160 kilometres into Austria. Two huge Russian armies advanced into Germany, pushing back the screen of defenders led by General Ludendorff. This was not difficult, for most German troops were busy with the Schlieffen Plan in France. Soon, however, the Germans recovered and hit back.

Ludendorff decided to attack. Moving quickly by rail, and using information from uncoded Russian radio messages, he brilliantly surrounded and trapped General Samsonov's

Russia and the Eastern Front, 1914–1915

army at Tannenberg. A German officer described the slaughter:

The sight of thousands of Russians driven into huge lakes or swamps to drown was ghastly, and the shrieks and cries of the dying men he will never forget. So fearful was the sight of these thousands of men with their guns, horses and ammunition, struggling in the water that, to shorten their agony, they turned the machine-guns on them. But even in spite of that, there was movement seen among them for a week after. And the mowing down of the cavalry brigade at the same time, 500 mounted men on white horses, all killed and packed so closely together that they remained standing.

64

Russian troops surrender to the Austrians in 1915

Tannenberg was a Russian disaster. The artillery had no shells to hit back with. Officers were baffled by orders followed by counter-orders. Aircraft lacked enough petrol to help. As a result the Russians lost about 180 field guns, about 70,000 men were killed or wounded, and about 50,000 were taken prisoner. General Samsonov was so ashamed that he committed suicide.

Then with additional troops now arriving by train from France, Ludendorff rapidly moved his entire army northwards by rail to deal with the second Russian force, led by General Rennenkampf. It was surprised and totally defeated in the Battle of the Masurian Lakes. Here another 100,000 Russians were killed or wounded. The steamroller had been destroyed. There was relief and rejoicing in Germany, and great worry in France.

Replacing the men from Russia's huge population of 165 million was not difficult, but by 1915 the shortage of weapons and shells was

very serious. Russian artillery often had no shells at all for days on end.

During most of 1915 the Germans remained on the defensive in France while the British and French lost precious men in useless attacks. On the Eastern Front, however, where trenches stretched for 1,120 kilometres and were not so heavily protected, attack was a more realistic idea. In May 1915 the Germans and Austrians launched a huge offensive around the town of Gorlice (see the map on page 64). Soon the Russians were driven out of Germany and far back into Russia itself. Bewildered Russian garrisons collapsed and surrendered as German cavalry and guns moved quickly over the wide rolling Russian plains.

Only winter saved Russia from total defeat, and cheated the Germans of a breakthrough. Snow and ice prevented further movement until spring, but it also brought great hardship for men in trenches. Hundreds died of cold as they huddled together for warmth in frozen dug-outs. Russian civilians were short of food, which had been commandeered by Russian or German troops. Roads, bridges, cities and villages lay ruined and broken all over the Eastern Front, and about 2 million Russian men were casualties. It seemed that by the end of 1915 Russia was already defeated.

Nevertheless, 1916 saw a huge Russian counter-attack, led by the brilliant General Brusilov. Preparing in great secrecy, he gradually re-equipped the shattered Russian armies, partly with weapons sent from Britain and France. Then in June he attacked, driving deep into Austrian territory. Much of the land lost in 1915 was regained. Thousands of prisoners were taken and the fierce Cossack cavalry caused havoc by destroying supplies and reinforcements. It really seemed as if Brusilov had forced a breakthrough and saved Russia.

At this moment the Germans were besieging Verdun (page 48). Brusilov's attack forced them to send troops to help their Austrian allies and this helped save the French. But the arrival of more Germans saved the Austrians, and Russia's breakthrough was halted. Gradually the tide turned and once again the Russians began to retreat. Weapons were abandoned and could not be replaced. Shells and bullets ran out. Hospitals ran out of medicines. It was the same old story once again.

For a time there had been great hope and enthusiasm as Brusilov's armies advanced, but now the long-suffering troops, and their hungry families back home, faced the winter of 1916 with broken spirits and growing anger. Little did anyone realise that the following year would be the most important in Russian history. (See Chapter 12.)

Turkey joins the war

As we saw in Chapter 2, Turkey, Austria and Germany had formed a close friendship before 1914. Turkey and Austria shared the Slav problem and both opposed Russia. Germany had modernised the Turkish Army, and was still building the Berlin-Baghdad Railway when the war began in 1914.

Turkey was not a member of the Triple Alliance and had no obligation to fight, but several factors helped push her into war. The Turkish Empire was old and weak, and recently several Slav peoples had made Turkey look feeble by winning independence from Turkish rule. Here was a chance to find military glory again, and to settle old arguments with Russia. Then in August 1914 two German warships, the *Goeben* and the *Breslau*, fleeing from British warships in the Mediterranean Sea, appeared in the harbour at Constantinople, the Turkish capital (now Istanbul). They came in peace, seeking safety in a neutral harbour; but then they turned their huge guns towards the city. The threat was enough—Turkey joined the war on the German side.

One early result of this was a British and Indian attack near Baghdad, in Mesopotamia, in 1915. Part of the Turkish Empire sprawled across the Middle East towards the Persian Gulf, where Britain owned vital oil wells. Fearing an attack on these oil supplies, Britain sent troops to attack the Turks. For a time they advanced successfully through the scorching Mesopotamian desert, but then they were cut off and besieged for four and a half months at Kut. Thirst and disease killed thousands of British and Indian troops before about 10,000 survivors finally surrendered in April 1916 and were marched off into captivity. Turkey had become another problem for the Allies to face.

The attack at Gallipoli

By early 1915 Russia desperately needed help from her allies after defeats at Tannenberg and the Masurian Lakes. The Allies had to send supplies to keep the Russians going—but how? The sea routes to Russia were either too long or frozen over for much of the year. The only real possibility was to push through Turkey to the Black Sea and the Russian port of Odessa.

The map of Turkey shows that the only sea route from the Mediterranean to the Black Sea passes first through the channel called the Dardanelles into the Sea of Marmara, and then through the Bosporus past Constantinople into the Black Sea. Any Allied ships ferrying supplies to Russia would have to pass through

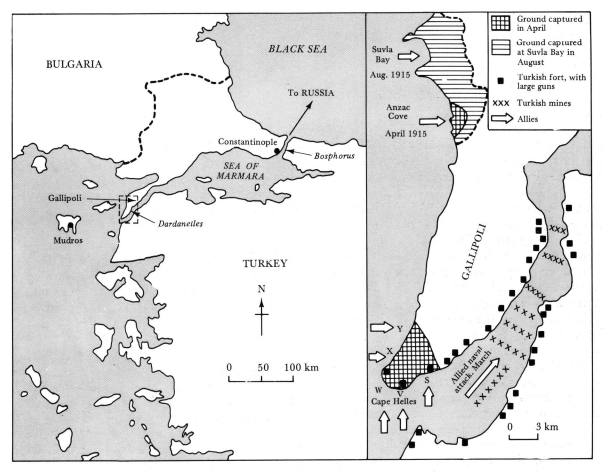

The attack at Gallipoli, 1915

these two narrow straits, both heavily defended by Turkish forts. Obviously these would have to be destroyed first, so it was decided to attack the Dardanelles in order to help Russia later. With the forts captured, troops would march to Constantinople and take the city, and the supply ships would get through to Odessa.

In 1915 Britain could not spare many troops for such a plan. The BEF was too busy in France and Lord Kitchener's new army of volunteers was not ready. Instead, Winston Churchill, the First Lord of the Admiralty, urged a naval attack. British and French battleships would sail through the Dardanelles, destroying the forts with their huge guns as they went.

The naval attack began on 18 March 1915 with a fleet of old battleships advancing cautiously into the narrow channel. No one knew

that rows of underwater mines had been laid by the Turks until the French battleship *Bouvet* hit one at 2.00 pm and sank. Then the *Inflexible* hit another, and 3 minutes later so did the *Irresistible*. With the attack in confusion, HMS *Ocean* went to help the *Irresistible* and also hit a mine. Meanwhile the French ship *Gaulois* was badly damaged by gunfire from the shore forts. These heavy losses forced Admiral de Robeck, who was in charge of the attack, to abandon the plan, and the remaining ships withdrew. Nothing had been achieved. Some forts had been destroyed, but now the Turks were alerted to the attack plan and any chance of surprise was gone.

It was decided that troops must now be used to capture the Turkish guns from the landward side. They would attack the west coast of the

'Y' Beach at Gallipoli. In the distance lies Cape Helles. The troops were expected to attack up these steep slopes

Gallipoli peninsula, cross overland, and capture the forts from behind. Britain could not spare many troops, but fortunately the Australian and New Zealand Army Corps (or ANZACs), on their way to France, had reached Egypt. These men were diverted to Gallipoli to combine with British troops.

A British supply base was created at Mudros, a Greek island near Gallipoli. Then the ANZAC troops arrived, but found their equipment wrongly packed. The resulting confusion warned the Turks of a coming military attack, and led by their German commander, Liman von Sanders, they strengthened their defences for an invasion.

The attack itself was badly planned. General Sir Ian Hamilton selected landing areas without even checking if they were suitable—in fact they were useless. On 25 April 1915, British troops landed on five beaches at Cape Helles, while Australian and New Zealand soldiers landed further north at a bay soon called Anzac Cove. Both groups were supposed to move rapidly inland to capture the forts before the Turks had time to react. This did not happen.

At 'Y' beach there were no Turkish defenders. Once they had landed, the troops just sat around waiting for instructions, losing precious time until the enemy arrived and it was too late to advance. At 'X' beach the Turks, terrified by a heavy naval bombardment, were easily overpowered, but when the British reached the top of the nearest hills they again stopped to await further orders. The same happened at 'S' beach. At 'W' beach barbed wire and determined Turkish troops held up the British attack on the beach itself. But when the defenders were eventually overpowered the British dug trenches to prepare for Turkish counter-attacks. Everywhere, local officers, who should have been pressing on while the Turks were still disorganised, waited instead for more instructions. Meanwhile Sir Ian Hamilton was on a battleship well offshore.

The worst fighting was at 'V' beach. Here an old steamer, the *River Clyde*, had been specially

Anzac Cove some time after the landings. In the background are piles of supplies, and dug-outs cluster up the steep hillside. The men in the foreground are Anzacs wearing their distinctive hats

converted to carry lots of troops close in to the shore. Sandbags and steel plates protected the decks from gunfire and special square holes were cut in the hull to let the men out. John Masefield described the scene:

The plan was to beach her as near the shore as possible, and then drag or sweep the lighters, which she towed, into position between her and the shore, so as to make a kind of boat bridge from her to the beach. When the lighters were so moored as to make this bridge, the entry ports were to be opened, the waiting troops were to rush out on to the external platforms, run from them to the lighters, and so to the shore . . . but almost as she grounded when the picket boats with their tows were ahead of her, only 20 or 30 yards (18 or 27 metres) from the beach, every rifle and machine-gun in the castle, the town above it, and in the curved, low, strongly trenched hill along the bay, began a murderous fire upon the ship and boats. There was no question of their missing . . .

Many were killed in the water, many who were wounded, were swept away and drowned; others, trying to swim in the fierce current, were drowned by the weight of their equipment. But some reached the shore, and these instantly doubled out to cut the wire entanglements, and were killed, or dashed for the cover of a bank of sand or raised beach which runs along the curve of the bay. Those very few who reached this cover were out of immediate danger, but they were only a handful . . . When day dawned, the survivors of the landing party were crouched under the shelter of the sandbank; they had had no rest; most of them had been fighting all night; all had landed across the corpses of friends . . . The fleet opened a terrific fire upon the ruins of the fort and village, and the landing party went forward again, fighting from bush to bush and from stone to stone, till the ruins were in their hands. Shells still fell among them, single Turks, lurking under cover, sniped them and shot them; but the landing had been made good, and 'V' beach was secured to us.

If anything the attack at Anzac Cove was even worse than this. The troops expected a flat landing area but as dawn came they found high cliffs facing them—they were landing in the wrong bay. As they struggled ashore a terrible fire rattled down from the hills around. Everything was chaos. Officers lost touch with men. Signals failed. Some of the troops crept up narrow gullies in the hills and fought with the Turks, but even where the defenders were driven off, no one had orders to keep pushing inland. Soon the Turks returned with reinforcements and, as at Cape Helles, the troops were pinned down by gunfire in a small area beside the coast. The troops had managed to get ashore, but the plan had failed.

Living at Gallipoli

Life at Gallipoli soon became a struggle for survival. In some places the Turks had positioned themselves in trenches that were only 9 metres away from the British troops. This was to prevent the Royal Navy from shelling, for fear of hitting their own men. Each side could hear the other talking. They could smell cooking and see cigarette smoke rising above the parapets, but it was also close enough to lob a hand grenade over and sentries had to be constantly alert.

In summer the heat and dust were dreadful. Water was extremely scarce and had to be carried by mules in cans from supply ships. Water

Anzac troops in a trench at Gallipoli. The man in the foreground is using a sniperscope—a rifle fitted to a frame, with an angled mirror. A string runs from the trigger to the man's hand as he waits patiently for a Turk to show himself. Another soldier watches through a trench periscope

Winter mud at Anzac Cove. An ambulance struggles through the slime

wells were guarded to prevent troops from raiding them. Flies were everywhere, smothering every scrap of food and causing widespread dysentery. Men soon grew weak and had to be sent to hospital ships waiting offshore. Of seven Anzac battalions examined in September 1915, 78 per cent of the men had dysentery and 64 per cent had skin sores.

For the Turks this was a Holy War, a struggle to drive out Christian invaders from Muslim Turkey. Time and again the Turks charged downhill at the Allies and were slaughtered by Vickers machine-guns. Sometimes the fighting became a desperate hand-to-hand struggle. The Anzac and British troops came to admire the great courage of the Turks. Meanwhile the fighting area became littered with corpses, rotting in the hot weather. The stench became so unbearable that temporary cease-fires were sometimes arranged while both sides buried the bodies. Then the killing started all over again.

Clearly this stalemate could not go on. Russia was desperate for help, so in August a new attack was made on Gallipoli. The landing area was at Suvla Bay, north of Anzac Cove.

Thousands of British and Anzac troops landed successfully on a flat shore—but then they settled down to brew tea, sunbathe or swim in the sea and by the time they moved on the Turkish General, Mustafa Kemal, had organised the defences. This new attempt was another failure and resulted simply in another army being pinned down in a small area. Meanwhile diseases continued to spread among the men, and many of them suffered from sunstroke.

There was one success story at Gallipoli. Several British submarines managed to slip through nets and minefields from the Dardanelles into the Sea of Marmora, where they did great damage. In all, 1 Turkish battleship, a destroyer, 5 gunboats, 11 transport ships (including one carrying 6,000 troops), 44 cargo ships, 184 sailing ships, coastal railways and trains, shore buildings and other targets were destroyed by 13 British submarines, of which 8 were also sunk. Commander Nasmyth even sank a transport ship inside Constantinople harbour. However, these successes did not bring victory any closer at Gallipoli.

Winter came. The dust and heat turned to mud and snow. Water now poured down the hills into the Allied trenches. Blizzards swept over men without overcoats, huddled together for warmth, caking them with freezing mud and ice. On 28 November, later called 'Frozen Foot Day', the cold reached its worst. Men simply died where they slept. By then 15,000 had died of exposure and a long queue of limping, frostbitten troops straggled down to the shore, shuffling through the sleet and exploding shells. Any chance of success had disappeared.

Sir Ian Hamilton was sacked and replaced by General Monro. He quickly decided to call off the attack, and a remarkable escape plan was prepared for the men trapped at Gallipoli. Suvla Bay and Anzac Cove were evacuated first. From 12 December, groups of men were secretly led at night from their trenches to waiting boats and quietly ferried away. Blankets were laid along tracks to deaden the sound of boots. Mules had sacking tied round their hooves. Horses which could not be taken off had their throats cut. Supplies were destroyed with acid.

Those who remained tried to deceive the Turks by lighting extra cooking fires and firing rifles up and down the deserted trenches. Then on 21 December the last troops slipped away, leaving the Turks to discover their departure next morning: 83,000 men had escaped without a single death.

The same happened soon after at Cape Helles. By 7 January over 15,000 men had been secretly evacuated. Suddenly the Turks attacked the remaining 19,000 but they were driven off in a fierce battle. Then to the relief of the British troops, the Turks refused to attack again—why bother, when the Allies were leaving anyway? So the operation went on until 3.45 am on 9 January when the last boat left. Ten minutes later the remaining stores blew up. Gallipoli was over.

Of the 410,000 British or Anzac troops who fought in the campaign, 213,980 died, just under three-quarters of them from disease. About 300,000 Turks also died. Nothing had been achieved.

Lawrence of Arabia

For centuries Turkey had ruled over the Arab tribes of the Middle East. These people hated the Turks and now offered to help the Allies. In

An Arab patrol. These troops are from Lawrence of Arabia's desert army

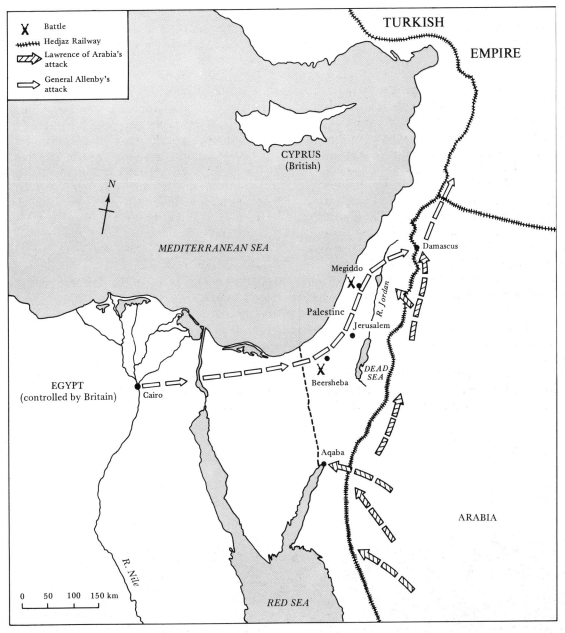

Key

X Battle

Hedjaz Railway

Lawrence of Arabia's attack

General Allenby's attack

TURKISH
EMPIRE

CYPRUS
(British)

N

MEDITERRANEAN SEA

Damascus

Megiddo

Palestine

R. Jordan

Jerusalem

*DEAD
SEA*

EGYPT
(controlled by Britain)

Cairo

Beersheba

Aqaba

ARABIA

R. Nile

0   50   100   150 km

RED SEA

The fighting in the Middle East

return they were promised freedom in their own desert homelands after Turkey was defeated. From 1914 to 1916 more and more Arab tribes followed their sheiks to war against Turkey.

Britain helped by shelling and air bombing Turkish shore forts, and by sending medicines and weapons. But the various Arab tribes really needed to be organised properly. In particular, a vital railway which ran through the Hedjaz Desert, enabling Turkish troops to reach the area quickly, had to be destroyed. A British army was gathered at Cairo in Egypt. Led by General Allenby, they prepared to attack into Palestine, while Major T. E. Lawrence was sent to meet the Arabs in the desert.

73

Although a Christian and a European, Lawrence was accepted by the Arabs. He learned their customs and language. He dressed like an Arab and learned to ride a camel. Above all, he was a brave fighter, which the Arabs admired. Soon he was leading them in attacks on the Hedjaz railway, blowing up bridges, ambushing Turkish troops and wiping out isolated garrisons before disappearing back into the desert. These hit-and-run attacks were a great nuisance to the Turks, and 'Lawrence of Arabia' became a legend.

Gradually the Arab forces pushed deeper into enemy territory and the fort at Aqaba was taken. Meanwhile General Allenby's army also advanced into Palestine. They broke through the Turkish army at Beersheba and in December 1917 captured Jerusalem. In another battle, Allenby's army defeated the Turks at Megiddo, helped by a diversionary attack by the Arabs. In October 1918 the two armies led by Lawrence and Allenby reached Damascus. Most Arab lands once ruled over by Turkey were now free.

Meanwhile a new attack was also made in Mesopotamia, where a British army had been forced to surrender at Kut in 1916 (page 66). This attack was more successful and penetrated far up the valleys of the Tigris and Euphrates rivers. Baghdad was captured and by October 1918 the Allies were at the borders of Turkey itself.

Italy joins the war

The Italians did not declare war with their German and Austrian allies in 1914. This was because Italy had close ties with Britain and France and did not want to fight against friends. Instead, the Italians decided to stay neutral. Of course the British now tried hard to persuade the Italians to join their side, for an ally to the south would help encircle Germany and force German troops away from the main fighting area in France. The Italians, like the Germans, longed for an impressive empire, especially around the Mediterranean Sea. Britain promised parts of Austria and Turkey, and so in April 1915 the Italians joined the Allies.

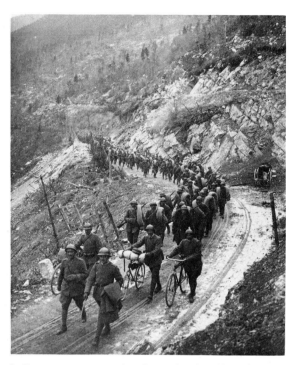

Italian troops retreating from the Austrians in 1917

Most of the fighting was against Austria, in the high snowy Alps of north Italy. Special mountain troops were often used—expert skiers and climbers—as a strange war began high among the clouds. Cable cars were used to ferry wounded men downhill. Machine-guns were dragged onto mountain peaks to prevent men from advancing along valleys.

Italian troops also crossed the border into the valley of the River Izonzo, but here they were checked by determined Austrian troops. Eleven battles were fought but the Italians made no more progress. Then in 1917, with German help, the Austrians attacked and destroyed the Italians at Caporetto. British and French troops were rushed to Italy as Austrian troops advanced, driving back those Italians who fought on.

In 1918 the Allies stopped the Austrian advance at Vittorio Veneto and the war ended soon after: 460,000 Italians died and another 500,000 were maimed for life. A total of 400,000 Austrians were also killed. Most Italians wished they had never joined the war.

9 The War at Sea

So far, the story of the First World War has been one of great land battles. What of the sea? You will remember from page 11 that before the war began, both Britain and Germany were racing to build battleships. What happened to the mighty dreadnoughts during the war?

The British Navy was certainly ready when war began. Winston Churchill, the First Sea Lord, had the entire fleet at its sea battle-stations before Britain even declared war. One of the first things he did was to order a naval blockade of Germany. This meant stopping all ships heading for German ports and turning back or sinking any found to be carrying food or supplies like oil or steel or chemicals. This blockade went on with great effect all through the war, gradually starving Germany of vital supplies. About 12,000 ships were intercepted while fewer than eighty slipped through. You will read on page 110 how this helped defeat Germany.

A remarkable stroke of luck also gave Britain a great advantage over Germany. Early in the war the German cruiser *Magdeburg* was sunk by Russian ships in the Baltic Sea. The body of a German officer was later found clutching a naval code book. From then on the British were able to decode German naval radio signals, and knew when enemy ships were leaving port.

To begin with, both sides were nervous. They feared new weapons like the torpedo and the mine, which could sink even a dreadnought. As a result, while small warships like destroyers and gunboats patrolled the English Channel and the North Sea, the big battleships mostly stayed in port. The dreadnoughts were anchored at Scapa Flow, a protected and sheltered bay in the Orkney Islands. The battle-cruisers were at Cromarty, in the Moray Firth, and Rosyth in the Firth of Forth. The German 'High Seas Fleet' spent most of the time at its base in Wilhelmshaven.

The first sea battles

One vital task for the Navy at the very start of the war was to find and destroy all German warships scattered around the world, before they could reach home. Most German ships dashed for the nearest neutral port, where they stayed rusting until the end of the war. This cut German colonies off from home and robbed German factories of important supplies. However some ships did try to get back to Germany.

The government was particularly concerned about the powerful warship the *Goeben*, which was sailing with the *Breslau* in the Mediterranean when war began. Realising that these vessels could sink many British ships carrying goods from India or Australia through the Suez Canal, the Navy had started shadowing them even before the war began. However the two German ships managed to escape, though only to Turkey (page 66), and they did little to help the German war effort after this.

Another serious German threat was the Pacific Squadron, based at Kiaochow in China. One of these ships was the fast light cruiser *Emden*, commanded by Captain Müller. On 7 August 1914 the *Emden* set off on her last, but famous, voyage. Müller knew that Allied warships would be looking for him, so he disguised his ship with an extra funnel and then sailed boldly into the Indian Ocean. There is not space to tell the full story of her adventures here—she sank fifteen ships and captured another eight in just seven weeks. Finally the *Emden* was caught by the more powerful Australian cruiser *Sydney*. After a blazing battle in which 142 of the 394 men on board were killed, the German ship was finally battered into defeat.

Meanwhile the remaining ships from the German Pacific Squadron, led by Admiral von Spee, set off for Germany across the Pacific Ocean. Off the coast of Chile, in South America, they met four old British battleships led by Admiral Craddock. As the sun set the British were silhouetted perfectly against the sky. Two of the ships were destroyed in the battle of Coronel and 1,440 British sailors were lost. It was the first British naval defeat for over a hundred years. Von Spee was now approaching the South Atlantic, so a force of modern warships was rushed to the British base in the Falkland Islands. Five weeks later von Spee's ships arrived to raid this base and were surprised by the British ships. Two German battle-cruisers and two light cruisers were destroyed; 1,800 German sailors died for the

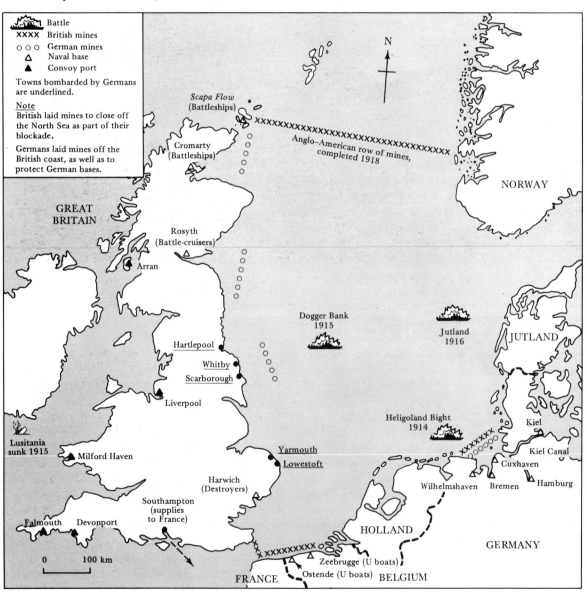

The war at sea, 1914–1918

Admiral Beatty's battle-cruisers ready for action at Rosyth, near the Forth Bridge. This photograph, taken on board the HMS Queen Elizabeth, *shows two of the vessel's eight huge 15-inch guns. The observation balloon in the distance was probably looking out for U-boats*

loss of only 30 British. The German Pacific Squadron was now destroyed.

Early battles in the North Sea

There were few battles in the North Sea, for both sides were anxious to keep their ships intact. For Britain especially, one defeat at sea would be worse than anything on land. Admiral Jellicoe, commander of the British 'Grand Fleet', was the only man who 'could lose the war in an afternoon', as Winston Churchill said. Nevertheless, the first battle took place only three weeks after the war began.

Fast British destroyers, deliberately sailing close to the German coast, were chased by a patrol of more powerful German cruisers—straight towards the huge battle-cruisers of Admiral Beatty's ships from Rosyth, waiting further out at sea. The trap worked beautifully. Three enemy cruisers and a destroyer were sunk before they could turn and flee out of range. Over a thousand German sailors died for the loss of fewer than fifty British, in what was called the Battle of Heligoland Bight.

The British public was much encouraged by this success, and Admiral Beatty became a popular hero. It seemed to prove that Britain would be safe from German attacks. Nevertheless, Britain relied so much on protection from the Navy that any battle was risky, and from now on the ships remained mostly in port. Somehow the Germans had to persuade the Royal Navy to come out again.

Part of Admiral Jellicoe's First Battle Squadron. These huge battleships are sailing in 'line astern' formation with their gun turrets all pointing in the same direction. Battleships before HMS Dreadnought *could not do this*

As the long nights of winter 1914 arrived, the Germans tried a new plan. On 16 December German battle-cruisers suddenly appeared off Hartlepool, on the North Sea coast. It was 8.10 am, and most people were having breakfast when the first shells came crashing down, killing many people, including women and children. Whitby and Scarborough were also shelled that day, and about 500 innocent civilians were killed or wounded before the German ships disappeared.

The public was outraged—where had the Royal Navy been? This was just what the Ger-

mans wanted, for the idea was to force the British Navy to stretch its fleet as a protective chain right along the North Sea coast. This would allow the German fleet to sink single British ships without having to face up to the full 'Grand Fleet'. The Royal Navy did not fall for this plan, but it did increase patrols in the North Sea, trying to catch German ships on their way to another bombardment.

Soon this decision paid off. On 24 January 1915, using information gained from intercepting German radio signals, Admiral Beatty's ships caught a strong German force well out in the North Sea where there was no chance of escape. Here at last was a battle between the mighty dreadnought battle-cruisers of both sides. Soon the huge guns of HMS *Lion*, Beatty's flagship, were blazing away at the enemy as the German ships turned for home. Two German battle-cruisers were destroyed as the British ships pressed home their attack, but then HMS *Lion* was damaged and had to slow down, and the remaining German ships escaped. This was the Battle of the Dogger Bank. Once again Beatty came home a great hero.

The Battle of Jutland, 1916

Despite the battles of Heligoland Bight and the Dogger Bank, neither side had yet sent its full fleet out to sea. The risks were too great. But then on 31 May 1916, HMS *Galatea*, patrolling

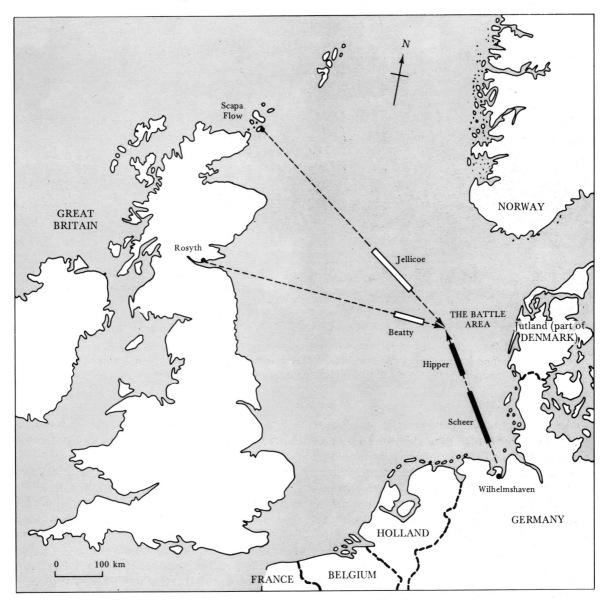

The Battle of Jutland, 1916

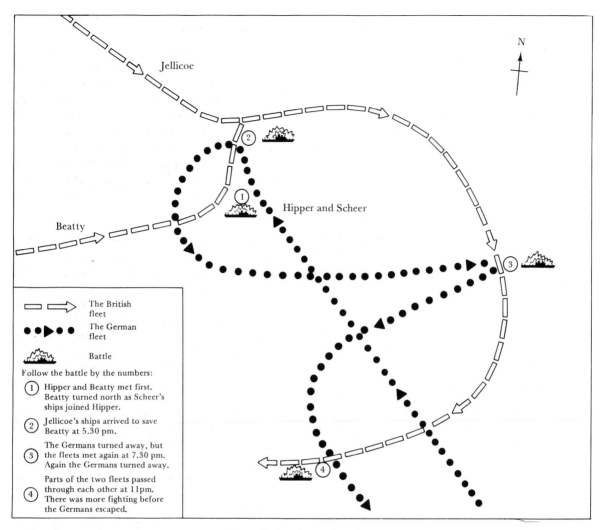

Legend:

- □ ⇨ The British fleet
- ●●▶●● The German fleet
- 🔥 Battle

Follow the battle by the numbers:

① Hipper and Beatty met first. Beatty turned north as Scheer's ships joined Hipper.

② Jellicoe's ships arrived to save Beatty at 5.30 pm.

③ The Germans turned away, but the fleets met again at 7.30 pm. Again the Germans turned away.

④ Parts of the two fleets passed through each other at 11pm. There was more fighting before the Germans escaped.

Map labels: Jellicoe, N, Beatty, Hipper and Scheer

How Jutland was fought

the North Sea, spotted an enemy destroyer. Gradually ninety-eight more ships appeared —the whole German 'High Seas Fleet' was at sea. Within an hour Jellicoe's battleships from Scapa Flow and Beatty's battle-cruisers from Rosyth were racing out for battle.

On the German side were twenty-two modern dreadnought battleships led by Admiral Scheer, and five modern battle-cruisers led by Admiral Hipper. In addition there were many smaller cruisers and destroyers to screen the larger ships. The British 'Grand Fleet' was larger, totalling 151 assorted warships. The overall fleet commander was Admiral Jellicoe, with twenty-eight powerful battleships in his section. Admiral Beatty led six battle-cruisers and four battleships. These were supported by dozens of cruisers and destroyers—smaller but faster than dreadnoughts, and armed with torpedoes which could sink battleships. The scene was set for the greatest sea battle in history.

Stage 1 (see map): Beatty's battle-cruisers arrived first, because they were faster and Rosyth was closer than Scapa Flow. At about 2.30 pm Beatty's flagship HMS *Lion* spotted

Hipper's battle-cruisers about 9 kilometres away and the mighty 13½-inch guns began firing. For over 2 hours the air was filled with belching black smoke, gun flashes, the choking smell of cordite and gunpowder and the noise of explosions and twisting metal, as both sides blazed away. As each salvo smashed into the ships there were cries of 'Fire parties!' or 'Stretchers!' as crews struggled to save their ships.

Then suddenly at 4.02 HMS *Indefatigable* blew up after a punishing bombardment from the German battle-cruiser *Von der Tann*. Over a thousand officers and men were killed by the explosion or drowned. It was a great loss, but Beatty knew that Jellicoe was on the way so he fought on. The German gunfire was very accurate, and soon came another disaster for the British. The First Gunnery Officer on the German battle-cruiser *Derfflinger* described it later:

> Since 16.24 pm every one of our salvoes had straddled the enemy. When the salvo fired at 16 hours, 26 minutes, 10 seconds fell, heavy explosions had already begun in the *Queen Mary*. First of all a vivid red flame shot up from her forepart. Then came an explosion forward which was followed by a much heavier explosion amidships, black debris of the ship flew into the air, and immediately afterwards the whole ship blew up with a terrific explosion. A giant cloud of smoke rose, the masts collapsed inwards, the smoke cloud hid everything and rose higher and higher. Finally nothing but a thick, black cloud of smoke remained where the ship had been.

Only seventeen men survived the explosion of the *Queen Mary*, but still Beatty fought on, waiting for the arrival of Jellicoe. Even his own ship *Lion* was taking a battering, as a young lieutenant on board later wrote:

> . . . a bloodstained Sergeant of Marines appeared on the bridge. He was hatless, his clothes were burnt and he seemed to be somewhat dazed. I asked him what was the matter; in a tired voice he replied: ' "Q" turret has gone, sir. All the crew are killed, and we have flooded the magazine.' I looked over the bridge. The armoured roof of 'Q' turret had been folded back like an open sardine tin, thick yellow smoke was rolling up in clouds from the gaping holes and the guns were cocked up awkwardly in the air.

Ninety-eight men were killed in one turret by one shell from the German battle-cruiser *Lutzow*. Sparks had showered down into the magazine room where the shells were kept, threatening the ship with an explosion as dreadful as the others, but a dying Royal Marine officer ordered the magazine to be flooded just in time and almost certainly saved the ship. This ended the first stage of the battle. At this point the German fleet seemed to be winning.

Stage 2: Suddenly the great battleships of Admiral Scheer's fleet appeared and now Beatty was in serious trouble. He turned north, trying to lure them towards Jellicoe's ships. The Germans followed, and fell into the trap. There on the horizon appeared the twenty-eight battleships from Scapa Flow. As shells whistled overhead to land among the German ships, Beatty knew that he had been saved just in time.

Stage 3: As the German ships came under heavy fire from Jellicoe they still fought back. At about 6.30 pm the battle-cruiser *Invincible* was hit. Sparks reached the gun magazines and she exploded. By now, however, the Germans had also suffered many hits, so in a brilliantly worked move which they had often practised, the entire German fleet did an about turn and tried to sail off at full speed for home. German destroyers raced about making a smoke screen and threatening to attack the British fleet with torpedoes—enough to delay the chase. Later Jellicoe did follow, and again Scheer's vessels did an about turn, but then evening came and in the gloom the Germans slipped away.

Stage 4: During the night part of the two fleets passed through each other again, as the British tried to cut the Germans off from home. Again there was heavy fighting and the darkness was lit up by criss-crossing searchlights and fiery explosions, but when early morning came the seas were empty. The Germans had escaped and the battle was over.

Many medals were won at Jutland. Among the best known was the Victoria Cross given to Boy First Class John Cornwell, part of a gun crew on the cruiser HMS *Chester*. Admiral Beatty wrote:

> Mortally wounded early in the action, he nevertheless remained standing alone at a most exposed post quietly awaiting orders with the gun's crew dead and wounded all around him. His age was under sixteen and a half years. I regret that he has since died, but I recommend his case for special recognition in justice to his memory and as an acknowledgement of the high example set by him.

Who won the battle of Jutland? The British lost 3 battle-cruisers (all from explosions in the magazines), 3 cruisers and 8 destroyers—14 ships and about 6,000 men. The Germans lost 1 battleship (sunk by a torpedo during the night), 1 battle-cruiser, 4 light cruisers and 5 destroyers—a total of 13 ships and about 2,500 men. Clearly the Germans did better. German gunnery was also better—about half of all big shells scored hits compared with about a third for the British ships. Nevertheless, from then on the German fleet rarely went to sea again, and the Royal Navy was left in control of the North Sea. As a result, the Germans turned to a new weapon—the submarine.

Submarine warfare

In 1914 the submarine was still a fairly new idea. Some Royal Navy men called it a 'damned un-English weapon' because it attacked unseen, sneaking up on its victim. The

Jack Cornwell VC. He was killed at the Battle of Jutland, aged only sixteen

The sinking of the Lusitania. *This drawing, made from eyewitness accounts of survivors, appeared in the* Illustrated London News *a few days later*

Germans had no such worries, and by 1914 the *Unterseeboot* or U-boat was able to attack British shipping with guns and torpedoes.

As an island, Britain was very vulnerable to attacks from U-boats. British farmers could not produce enough food for the whole population, and some crops like tea and sugar cane would not grow in such a cold climate anyway. In addition, Britain lacked oil, rubber and many other important industrial goods. These had to come from abroad, mainly from the British Empire, by ship. Early in the war the Germans realised that if they could sink enough ships, Britain could be forced to surrender, either from starvation or from a lack of war materials. U-boats were the obvious answer.

To begin with U-boats lurked in the Atlantic Ocean near Britain, waiting for likely targets. Having found a ship they would surface, stop the vessel by pointing a gun at it, search the cargo, allow the crew time to abandon ship, and then sink it with gunfire. Torpedoes were

not wasted if the gun could be used instead. Only Allied ships were sunk—neutral ships were not harmed.

This method did not work well, for there was no way of stopping neutral ships from unloading in British ports. So in February 1915 the Germans created 'war zones' round the entire British Isles. Germany warned the world that from now on, any ship from any country found in these war zones would be sunk. This was very unpopular and neutral countries protested strongly, but Germany was determined to cut Britain off.

In May 1915 the huge transatlantic liner *Lusitania* left New York bound for Liverpool. Despite posters published in America by the German Embassy warning people not to sail on British ships, nearly 2,000 passengers were on board. On 7 May the submarine *U20*, commanded by Captain Walther Schweiger, spotted the unmistakable vessel with its four red and black funnels sailing off southern Ireland in a war zone. Two torpedoes easily sank the liner. A total of 1,198 people, many of them women and children, including 128 Americans, were drowned. A world outcry followed, but the Germans treated Schweiger's crew as heroes, insisting that the *Lusitania* had been carrying war goods (an argument that has never been settled). Even so, America's anger that a passenger ship had been sunk without warning or a chance being given for women and children to escape, gained worldwide sympathy. Germany, fearing that America might even join the war on Britain's side, promised to stop attacking passenger ships. Ships were once again stopped and searched.

By March 1916 things had become more desperate for Germany. The attack at Verdun was going badly. Russia was not yet defeated and Italy had joined the Allied side. It was vital to defeat Britain quickly, so Germany began sinking ships from all countries, as before. Although it meant angering neutral countries, even America, the possibility of defeating Britain was worth the risk.

In 1917 this campaign of 'unrestricted U-boat warfare' was stepped up, and by May it was beginning to bite. So many ships were being sunk that Britain was down to only six weeks' supply of certain foods. At one point there was only four days' supply of sugar. Defeat for Britain was never closer during the whole war. Then two things happened which saved Britain. First, America declared war on Germany. (This is dealt with fully on page 107.) Second, Britain found ways of defeating the U-boats.

Defeating the U-boats

Several ideas were used to overcome the submarine threat. For example, steel anti-submarine nets were hung from floats across harbour entrances. A gap allowed ships through but submarines became entangled.

Mines were also used. These were large round metal containers packed with explosives. Several spikes or 'horns' stuck out—if a ship touched a horn, the mine would explode. Floating mines were a danger to ordinary ships but a 'curtain' of mines could also be placed below the surface at varying depths, ready to destroy any submarine. By 1918 both the English Channel and the North Sea had been closed off by rows of deadly mines, which helped prevent supplies reaching Germany. Meanwhile German mines were also laid off the British coast. Lord Kitchener was drowned when the ship he was sailing in struck a mine off the north of Scotland.

Some ships were fitted with hydrophones, or listening devices. Sounds travel easily under water and an operator with headphones could hear a nearby submarine engine. An experienced man could quickly spot a new noise through the sound of his own ship's engine, and sometimes he even knew roughly from which direction the submarine was approaching.

One of the most effective weapons was the depth charge. This was a container about the size of a large oil drum, packed with explosives. It was dropped into the sea above a suspected submarine and could be set to explode at any depth, sending a fountain of water high into the air. Usually several depth charges were dropped together, set to detonate at different depths in case the U-boat dived. If one went off close to a submarine the underwater shock waves were often enough to buckle or split the hull, drowning the men inside. Those not drowned would probably be in watertight compartments where they would suffocate as the air was used up. Usually wreckage or oil would float to the surface to tell the ship of its success.

Another well-known trick was the 'Q' ship, which both sides used. This looked like a harmless cargo vessel, but it carried powerful guns disguised as freight or even as cabins on deck. When a U-boat surfaced to search the ship (not wanting to waste a torpedo on such an easy target), the crew would wait until the enemy was on deck, making it impossible for the submarine to dive quickly. Then the dummy crates or cabins would suddenly collapse to reveal the guns. The U-boat would be destroyed before it could escape.

By far the most successful idea, however, was the introduction of convoys in June 1917. A convoy was a group of ships sailing together

The torpedo from a German U-boat strikes a British merchant ship

and protected by fast warships such as armed trawlers or destroyers fitted with hydrophones and depth charges. Sometimes airships cruised overhead, trying to spot submarines lurking just under the surface of the water. The speed of a convoy depended on the slowest ship, so some convoys were quicker than others. Protecting warships zig-zagged around to confuse any U-boats that might be near. Sometimes a 'Q' ship sailed behind the convoy, pretending to be a straggler which a U-boat captain might find a tempting target.

At first the Navy opposed the idea of convoys, fearing the loss of precious warships, but the Prime Minister, Lloyd George, insisted, and convoys were introduced. There was an immediate improvement and supplies began to reach Britain again. Meanwhile American shipyards replaced sunk vessels at a remarkable rate (495 were built in sixteen months), and American ships now also joined the convoys.

The facts speak for themselves. From June 1917 to November 1918, 16,539 ships sailed in convoys and only 154 were torpedoed. In addition, the crews of many torpedoed ships were rescued by other vessels from the same convoy, which would not have happened to a lone ship. Also, with the entry of America into the war, about 1,100,000 American troops crossed the Atlantic in convoys, of whom only 637 were drowned. Britain was saved. The U-boat menace had been defeated.

10 The War in the Air

The development of aircraft

Although the aeroplane had only been invented in 1903 it had made tremendous advances by 1914. The English Channel was crossed by the Frenchman Louis Bleriot in 1909 and suddenly the British government realised that Britain could no longer depend on the Navy alone for defence. She needed an air force. As a result the Royal Flying Corps (RFC) was formed in 1912. No other country began the war with a properly trained air force.

To begin with, aircraft were used only for reconnaissance work or 'spotting'. They reported the positions of enemy troops and guns, and at sea they hunted for ships, but they did not carry bombs or guns. One early success for these spotters was in reporting the 'gap' at the Battle of the Marne in 1914, which allowed the British Army to push into a space between two German armies.

The Germans did not like having their secret movements observed by aeroplanes and soon anti-aircraft guns were introduced. Some pilots from both sides also tried to shoot down enemy aircraft, but to begin with they could only take pistols with them and shoot at each other as they flew along. Some even tried to manoeuvre their planes directly above the enemy, from where they tried to drop bricks onto the pilot or the engine.

Eventually aeroplanes became strong enough to have a machine-gun fitted. The normal Vickers gun was far too heavy so early British planes had a Lewis gun fitted on the upper wing, which the pilot could fire and even reload as he flew. The bullets were packed into a flat round drum which slotted on top of the machine-gun. By 1915 most reconnaissance planes were armed. Among the best known spotters were the British Bristol Scout, the French Nieuport and the German Fokker Monoplane (which unlike most other aircraft, had only one set of wings).

In 1915 the Germans developed the 'interrupter gear'. This device sychronised the firing of a machine-gun with the turning of a propellor, enabling a gun to be fitted right in front of the pilot. This made it much easier to fire accurately. The new invention was fitted to the Fokker Monoplane and until mid-1916 the Allies were practically wiped out from the skies over Europe. It was a difficult time for the RFC for they had nothing good enough to take on the deadly Fokker Monoplanes with their interrupter gear.

One British idea was to fit a machine-gun behind the propellor, with steel plates or 'deflectors' fixed on the propellor blades so that bullets would ricochet away harmlessly. Some bullets bounced back into the engine, however, or even back at the pilot, and the idea was not a success. Eventually the British produced the 'pusher' plane, which had a propellor behind the pilot. Later the British captured a Fokker Monoplane and soon British planes were fitted with the same interrupter gear. The dominance of the Germans in the skies was ended.

Most planes with machine-guns were known as 'fighters' and by 1916 they were much faster and stronger than anything in 1914. Apart from shooting down other planes they had many other jobs, including shooting at enemy balloons and airships and 'straffing', or machine-gunning, ground targets such as large crowds of troops, trenches, artillery positions, fuel and ammunition dumps, bridges and supply railways. Very few pilots on either side ever delib-

A British 'pusher' plane. This is an FE2b with its engine behind the wings and between the struts which go to the tail. The pilot and the gunner sitting in front of him have a clear view forward

erately attacked unarmed civilian targets such as hospitals or fleeing civilian refugees. There were many different fighters, including the French Spad, the British Sopwith Camel and the German Albatross and Fokker D7.

Considering how new air warfare was in 1914, the improvements and inventions made in just four years were considerable. Planes in 1914 were literally stringbags (as they were nicknamed) built with wire, wooden struts and canvas round an unreliable engine. Pilots had no navigation instruments, no guns, no radio, no parachutes and had to use sign language to communicate with one another in flight. By the end of the war, planes were fast, streamlined, well armed, with a variety of helpful instruments, parachutes, and a wide selection of much more dependable engines—several aircraft even had two engines. Many could fly hundreds of kilometres on bombing missions and could carry bombs which would have been too heavy even to lift into the air in 1914. There were seaplanes, planes for landing on aircraft-carriers, planes with snow skis, others adapted for desert conditions and some with cameras for air photography.

Air battles

British pilots in particular were allowed to go on lone 'hunting patrols' but most French and German and some British pilots preferred to fly in groups or squadrons. When such groups met, the resulting jumble of planes was known as a 'dog-fight' and the sky was filled with a twisting, whirling mass of aeroplanes manoeuvring into position and shooting. The main aim was to get on the tail of an enemy, for it was easier to shoot at him from behind while he could not shoot back. If possible, additional tactical advantage was gained by diving with the sun behind you, so that the enemy would not see you coming until too late.

In a dog-fight great care had to be taken with the ammunition. A Lewis gun had only about 400-500 bullets per flight, which could be used up in about 50 seconds. Inexperienced pilots had to be trained not to fire in long bursts or they would soon run out of ammunition. Different aircraft also had flying weaknesses which could prove fatal in a dog-fight. The Sopwith Camel, for example, could flick very quickly to the right but only slowly to the left, so pursuing Germans would expect a pilot to twist away to the right and be ready for him. As a result two-seater aircraft became more important. While the pilot concentrated on flying, the observer–navigator could fire a machine-gun backwards in a dogfight, making it more difficult for the enemy to get on the tail. Eventually German pilots were given parachutes but the British were not, for it was claimed, very unfairly, that they would bale out at the first sign of trouble. British pilots were angry at being called cowards and many died in burning planes because they had no parachutes.

The pilots

Most pilots were well-educated young men, generally from well-to-do homes and public schools. Many were under twenty-one when they joined the RFC and few were over twenty-five. When they first went into action most pilots had flown no more than 30 hours in training, and perhaps no more than 6 by themselves, but they were very enthusiastic and undoubtedly very brave. They also had to be intelligent in a way that ordinary soldiers did not need to be, for all kinds of mechanical things could go wrong, even in the air, calling for instant snap decisions and ingenious repairs. Navigation also demanded brains and air fights required constant sharp wits.

The first air battle was always the most dangerous for a pilot. Most of them had never even fired a gun in the air during training—the nearest they got was shooting at a target from a speeding train. If they lived through this, their chances of survival improved with every additional scrap of experience gained in combat. Many did not make it—it was quite possible for a young man to leave school, be trained as a pilot, be sent to France, shoot down several planes, win several medals, and be killed, all before his twenty-first birthday.

The French system of 'aces' soon became popular, especially in the newspapers, though British officials never approved. The qualification was 5 confirmed 'kills', making a total of 537 British pilots who were aces. Of these heroes, only a few remain famous today. The most famous German was Baron Manfred von Richthofen, the 'Red Baron' (because he flew in a red plane), who was the war's top ace with 80 kills. Another German, Werner Voss, shot down 22 British planes in twenty-one days.

The most successful British pilot was Major Mick Mannock. Unlike most others, he really hated the Germans and once ruthlessly shot down 6 unarmed planes on a training flight. He had 73 kills when he was shot down in 1918. At his death he had been awarded a Victoria Cross (the highest British medal for bravery), three Distinguished Service Orders, and two Military Crosses.

The best-known Briton was undoubtedly Albert Ball, a shy public school boy from Nottingham. He joined the RFC aged only eighteen, won a VC, three DSOs and an MC, wrote regularly to his mother (for he was still just a boy), and was killed when only twenty. He thought nothing of taking on 6 or 7 enemy planes, shooting down 1 or 2, and then escaping in a bullet-ridden plane himself. He only flew

Major William Barker standing beside his Sopwith Camel

for four months but he shot down 43 enemy planes, a record at the time. Other Allied aces included the Canadian Billy Bishop (72 kills) and the French pilots Albert Fonck (75 kills) and Georges Guynemer (74 kills).

Many of these men were incredibly brave. The Canadian pilot William Barker, for example, once fought alone against more than 60 Germans all flying Fokker D7s, the finest plane in the war. Early in this battle his right thigh was almost cut off by bullets. Later, his left leg was also hit and his left elbow was shattered. Twice he fainted from pain and loss of blood, but he still shot down 4 Germans and managed to land his plane at 90 mph near some British trenches without its catching fire. It was riddled with over 300 bullet holes. Although he was unconscious for ten days, he eventually recovered and received a Victoria Cross from King George V.

Life on a flying field

RFC airfields were bleak and lonely places, often set among the monotonous flat fields in Flanders. The only relief from boredom was in drinking and music. These were frowned on by senior officers but squadron commanders tolerated them for there was no other way for a young man to relax after the great tension of a flight. Pilots were also allowed a curious variety of clothes—for a time there was no official uniform, and RFC pilots dressed in anything from army tunics and 'RFC maternity jackets' to fleece-lined leather jackets, woolly sweaters, silk scarves, woollen scarves, leather flying coats (buttoned or unbuttoned), gloves, riding breeches, ordinary trousers, shoes, sheepskin boots, riding boots, army 'puttees'—whatever they liked. Many items of clothing were chosen for warmth, for even in July it could be very cold in an open cockpit at 5,000 feet (1,540 metres).

Losses were small compared with those in the trenches. On average about 5,000 troops died each day in the trenches—about as many as died in the air during the entire war. As a result pilots were not filled with the same hatred of war and fear of death which troops felt. Most feared being burned alive in a crashed plane, but they did not see men being blasted and shell-shocked day after day, and they did not live in such awful conditions.

There were no Sunday church parades on airfields for pilots flew all week, weather permitting, and often lost track of weekends. There were also no medical centres and wounded men had to be taken to the nearest army field dressing-station by bumpy ambulance. Leave was also very irregular and seldom spent in Britain. It was a strain—but it was better than the trenches.

Air bombing

Between December 1914 and June 1917 there were 57 German aeroplane raids and 51 airship raids on Britain, mostly on London but also on industrial towns like Newcastle, Leeds, Manchester, Liverpool, Birmingham and even Glasgow. About 5,000 people were killed or wounded by German bombs. Because of improved defences from anti-aircraft fire (nicknamed 'archie') and fighter planes, the Germans switched to night attacks, especially

A squadron of British pilots (and dog) in 1918. The aircraft are SE5a Scouts, with Lewis guns fitted on the upper wings. Many famous aces, including Mick Mannock and James McCudden, used this plane because of its manoeuvrability in a dog-fight. The photograph also shows the variety of clothes worn even as late as 1918

A German Zeppelin. Most of the crew are housed in cabins below the hull, but notice the gunner standing on top

on London, which they reached by following the moonlit River Thames. Towards the end of the war the raids increased and from September 1917 to May 1918 there were 19 major attacks on London, during which over 300,000 people sought refuge in Underground railway stations.

The standard German bomber was the Gotha, which generally flew from Belgium. Plane losses were usually low—20 to 25 planes normally took part in a raid, of which 2 or 3 might be destroyed. Five were considered a heavy loss. In a typical raid on 7 July 1917, 24 Gothas set off; 2 dropped out with engine trouble while still over Belgium, a third developed engine trouble over England but bombed Margate before limping home, 1 was shot down over London and another crashed in Belgium on the way home. Over 100 British planes were used to attack this raid, yet 57 people were killed by the bombs dropped.

The Zeppelins or airships also frequently attacked Britain, but their raids generally did less damage, for their bombs could not be dropped accurately owing to the height they

had to maintain to keep out of reach of British fighters. As a result, Zeppelins also suffered few losses, but strong winds could blow them off course. In one famous raid, 11 Zeppelins set off from northern Germany into good weather over the North Sea, but were scattered by high winds over England. A total of 275 bombs were dropped, killing 36 civilians, but 4 airships were lost and a fifth crashed in Germany. One finished up over the Mediterranean and several more crossed over France and Belgium, thinking they were over the North Sea—an error made because the London guns deliberately did not fire, as part of a clever deception. This attack was soon nicknamed the 'Silent Raid'.

Using French and Belgian bases, the British bombed German towns in 1917–18. A favourite British bomber was the DH4, which could fly higher and faster than most enemy planes. Main targets were weapons factories and steelworks, some over 160 kilometres inside Germany; 24 towns were bombed in over 400 attacks. As in Britain there were many innocent victims—one raid killed 26 women and 126 children.

11 The Home Front

In previous wars, most ordinary British families were hardly involved, but this time things were very different.

Life for almost everyone was changed to some extent. It is said that every family lost a soldier relative in World War One, but the Germans also bombed many British towns and hundreds of civilians were killed too. Food was in short supply and farmers began to use every available space, changing the landscape considerably. Flowerbeds in parks, for example, were planted with vegetables instead. Many people also had to change jobs to help with the war effort, and quiet towns now found themselves manufacturing fighter aircraft or perhaps even poison gas.

We have seen how fighting areas in France, Russia, Italy and elsewhere were called 'fronts'. To many people it seemed as if Britain herself was really involved in the fighting too, and so people started to talk of the 'home front'.

Anti-German propaganda

From the first days of the war the British public was flooded with dreadful anti-German stories. It was vital to convince people that the Germans were barbarians or 'Huns', and popular newspapers like the halfpenny *Daily Mail* began to print horrific accounts of so-called German crimes. Refugees reaching Britain from Belgium were said to have brought tales of murder, rape and plunder—the 'Belgian Atrocities', as they were called. Several thousand Belgian civilians *were* shot by the Germans as hostages and many towns were looted by greedy soldiers, but in addition the newspapers published 'artists' impressions' of women being crucified, children having their

arms cut off by ugly, unshaven German soldiers, British prisoners being ill-treated, and so on. There were never any photographs, because most of these tales were untrue, invented simply to whip up strong anti-German feeling in Britain. On the whole this campaign worked.

THE ZEPPELIN RAIDS : THE VOW OF VENGEANCE
Drawn for 'The Daily Chronicle' by Frank Brangwyn ARA

'DAILY CHRONICLE' READERS ARE COVERED AGAINST THE RISKS OF BOMBARDMENT BY ZEPPELIN OR AEROPLANE

Anti-German propaganda. This example stresses how Zeppelin raids killed innocent people

Eager volunteers wait to join Lord Kitchener's New Army in 1915. This enthusiastic queue was outside Southwark Town Hall in London, but it was a scene repeated in every town and city. Notice the men's hats—they show middle- and working-class men mixed up together

A wave of hatred for anything German swept through Britain. Shops with German names were looted (many were in fact owned by Jews with German names). The Royal Family, which was of German descent, noted the public's feeling and changed its name from Saxe-Coburg to Windsor, while Queen Victoria's son-in-law changed his name from Battenberg to Mountbatten. All German citizens living in Britain were arrested as aliens and imprisoned for the duration of the war, in case they were spies. Even owners of dachshunds (a German breed of dog) were suspected of being German sympathisers!

War fever

When the war began in 1914 there was an amazing rush by young men to join the Army (see page 47). About 500,000 enlisted in August alone, in what has often been called a 'war fever'.

Why did so many men decide to join up? Obviously patriotism, the anti-German propaganda campaign, and the belief that they would be home by Christmas, were very important reasons. But there is more. Many saw their friends enlisting and did not want to be left out. Parents and girlfriends urged young men to

Daddy, what did _YOU_ do in the Great War?

A 'conscience' poster—probably the most famous to come from the war

enlist and called them cowards or refused to talk to them if they did not. Some young women pinned white feathers, a symbol of cowardice, on the lapels of men in the street not wearing a uniform. This was particularly cruel, for they sometimes unknowingly picked on men invalided out of the army with shell-shock, or men who had been prevented, perhaps by bad health, from enlisting.

Many men joined up without realising the horrors of trench life in store for them. Newspapers did not mention rats or trench foot. It is noticeable that as the war went on and wounded men came home with stories of what it was really like in the trenches, the number of volunteers began to drop.

'Conscience posters' began to appear. One typical poster said: 'You're proud of your pals in the Army of course! But what will your pals think of YOU?' In the music halls, where everyone went for entertainment in the days before radio or television, famous variety artists urged young men to join up by singing stirring patriotic songs like 'Rule Britannia'. Some even offered kisses to any young man who would enlist at a desk behind the stage. Sometimes the enthusiastic audience persuaded men to enlist.

There was also great confidence in victory in 1914. The troops marched off singing cheerful songs like 'Pack up your troubles in your old kit-bag and smile, smile, smile' or 'It's a long way to Tipperary'. Little did they know that soon they would be singing words like 'If you want the old battalion, we know where they are—they're hanging on the old barbed wire'.

There was even war fever among people who could not join up. When the government asked for donations to the troops there was a fantastic response. The public sent 232 million cigarettes and 16 million books, plus millions of dressings and bandages. Grannies all over Britain knitted 4 million pairs of socks, 2 million pairs of mittens and 2 million scarves for the troops. The whole population was caught up in the enthusiasm for the war.

The government takes charge

When the war began Britain was governed by the Liberal Party, led by the Prime Minister, Herbert Asquith. Right from the start it was important that the government should have additional powers to reorganise Britain for a war, so in August 1914 the Defence of the Realm Act (often nicknamed DORA) was passed. This allowed the government to make any regulations considered necessary for the safety of the country, even if they seemed very harsh and limited people's freedom. From then on a series of restrictions appeared which greatly changed many aspects of everyday life. For example, railways and docks now came under military law. Special constables, identified by special armbands, were appointed to help maintain law and order should the Germans ever invade Britain. All motor vehicles not required by the Army were to be made immobile if there was an invasion. Later in the war, air raid precautions were added to the list of regulations. All windows had to be blacked out (usually by heavy curtains or black paper) so that lights would not show at night. Special courts were set up to try anyone who disobeyed these new restrictions.

Another example was the 'Direction of Labour'. This meant that a man could be ordered to stop doing an unimportant job, and move to a different factory where his skills could be better used. Certain workers, such as miners, farmers, machine-tool operators and mechanics, were not allowed to join the Army because their skills were too important to waste—although many had already enlisted before this law was passed. Strikes in certain vital war industries were made illegal under the Munitions Act. Workers could be fined for striking, but they were guaranteed good minimum wages and could take any complaints to the Board of Trade. In peacetime, trade unions would never have accepted these restrictions, but they understood the need for them in wartime.

Censorship of the press began. Newspapers were not allowed to mention the disastrous battles being fought in France or elsewhere, or even to say much about air raids on Britain. Misleading descriptions of battles were common. Failures and high casualty rates were played down while small successes were exaggerated. One example was the Battle of the Somme which was a disaster from the very first day when the British lost 60,000 men. On the third day the *Daily Mirror's* headlines boasted: 'Great offensive continues—9,500 prisoners. British capture Fricourt and make progress east of Village and La Boisselle. French pierce foe second line.' There was no mention of the terrible slaughter. Meanwhile the German newspaper the *Frankfurter Zeitung* said: 'Anglo-French offensive—enemy's heavy losses and negligible gains. 15 enemy planes shot down.' A rather different version of the same battle.

Changes in the government

In May 1915 the Prime Minister decided it would be much better if the best men from all political parties could form a government

David Lloyd George. This remarkable Welshman put new heart into the British people after the Battle of the Somme, and led the nation to victory. He ordered the Army to use more machine-guns, and forced the Navy to introduce convoys. This photograph shows him making one of his fiery speeches

together to help Britain through the war. This new 'coalition government' included top Conservatives like Arthur Balfour and Bonar Law, and Arthur Henderson, the leader of the Labour Party, as well as several Liberals.

The energetic Lloyd George, the former Chancellor of the Exchequer, was put in charge of the Ministry of Munitions, with orders to increase shell production as fast as possible, following public outrage that there had not been enough shells during the British attacks of 1915 (see page 45).

During the next eighteen months this new government became rather unpopular. The attack at Gallipoli failed in 1915. Later attacks in France, such as the one at Loos in 1915, also failed, with heavy losses. Then came disaster in the Battle of the Somme. The coalition government had to take the blame.

In Dublin there was an attempted rebellion in April 1916 by Irishmen demanding independence from British rule. They hoped for German guns, but none came, and after heavy street fighting and a siege by the British Army of Dublin's General Post Office, the 'Easter Rising' was defeated. Fourteen republican leaders, including P. H. Pearse and James Connolly, were executed soon after.

As a result of these worrying events Asquith's coalition government was accused of weak leadership. What the country needed was someone with more drive and determination. A second coalition government was therefore formed in December 1916 and Lloyd George, who had shown great determination as Minister of Munitions, became the new Prime Minister. He turned out to be a great success as a wartime leader.

How everyday life changed

Everyone's life was altered by the war. Many towns, for example, changed over from peacetime industries to wartime work. Sheffield now made submarine periscopes. Gretna Green became the site of a huge ammunition factory. Warrington made barbed wire. Glasgow made aeroplanes while Runcorn found itself making most of the poison gas. Liverpool became the main port of arrival for Americans, Canadians and even Chinese labourers from Hong Kong. The Isle of Man had to find room for 50,000 German prisoners of war, while Southampton handled the arrival of more than a million sick and wounded soldiers from France. Many more towns were caught up in the war effort.

There were other changes too. No football league games were played during the war, and many footballers joined the Army. Outside Haymarket railway station in Edinburgh, for example, stands a war memorial to Heart of Midlothian players killed in the war. Pub licensing hours were shortened: Lloyd George said that Britain faced two dangers, Germany and Drink, so to protect young recruits and get more work done in factories, even shorter drinking hours were introduced. The government actually took over all pubs in certain areas, and beer was also watered down. As drinking declined, gambling and cinemas became more popular.

Nightclubs, once regarded as seedy, undesirable places, began to flourish, especially in London. It is said that there were 150 in the Soho district alone, mostly offering the new jazz music from America.

Attendance at church began to drop. On days of prayer churches were busy but otherwise they were not so full. People could not understand why God should permit such suffering and slaughter.

Food shortages and rationing

Britain depended heavily for some foods on imports, particularly from the Empire. All sugar, chocolate and cocoa, and most cheese, wheat, fruit and butter came by ship from overseas. Forty per cent of Britain's meat and even 36 per cent of her vegetables also had to be imported. German submarines made this food lifeline very precarious, but while reserve supplies lasted there was no real shortage in Britain. By 1916, however, the effects of the U-boat war were beginning to be felt.

Food queues appeared for the first time. The shortage of grain led to the introduction of a new bread made from real flour mixed with powdered potatoes or beans. This was called 'standard bread' and it was grey in colour. Margarine became a substitute for butter, and slogans like 'Save the Wheat and Help the Fleet—Eat Less Bread' appeared on posters, urging people not to waste food.

A great effort was made to grow more food in Britain itself. Hillsides and public parks were ploughed up. Waste land around towns and cities was rented out in small sections to tenement dwellers as allotments, on condition that they grew food, usually vegetables, until the war ended. City girls worked as volunteers on farms in a specially formed Land Army, which replaced farm-hands who had enlisted. Some girls found they actually enjoyed milking cows or ploughing with a horse. British Summer Time was introduced to create longer daylight working hours for these farm-workers. All of this did help a bit, but it was not enough and eventually some foods had to be rationed.

It began with sugar in December 1917, but meat and butter were added in early 1918, followed by products which contained sugar, such as jam, marmalade and chocolate biscuits. Tea was also added to the list eventually (and now the British public *really* complained

Women making hand grenades (called Mills bombs) at the Falkirk Iron Company in 1917. The girls in the foreground have their hair up under headscarves for safety when working the spinning lathes

about the Germans). Many other foods were in short supply and queues appeared at many markets, as shoppers searched for margarine, butter, meat and fish (578 British fishing boats were sunk during the war). On 21 January 1918 *The Times* reported that one butcher at Smithfield market had a queue of 4,000 people.

People received Ration Cards for foods like meat and sugar. These stated the shop where the holder could buy that item, and it was stamped each week by the shopkeeper to show that the week's supply had been bought. This meant that rich and poor were supposed to have an equal chance of obtaining foods in short supply. Mostly this worked, but a thriving 'black market' also provided more food for those who could pay for it.

Women help the war effort

Probably the most obvious change in Britain was the appearance of women in many jobs. Every woman, it seemed, wanted to 'do her bit'. The Pankhursts, powerful leaders of the Suffragettes before the war, now urged women to find work helping Britain win the war, and their demand for the vote was temporarily set aside. With so many men away fighting, women increasingly took over their jobs. Until 1914 only working-class women had worked, mostly in factories, but now they were joined by many middle- and upper-class women—the 'lilac and sun-bonnet brigade' as they were scornfully nicknamed, until people saw how hard they worked.

Nursing was the easiest way to find work but women soon found employment as secretaries, shop assistants, bus conductresses, taxi drivers, police, telephone operators, undertakers, office cleaners and in many other jobs usually done by men at that time. They also had to adapt to new ways—short hair or trousers, for example—and wealthy women not used to doing work had to overcome their horror of dirty hands and broken nails. Women now also appeared in uniform, from railway porters to ambulance drivers.

By July 1917 over 650,000 women were working in government offices alone. The Land Army took another 250,000. Engineering factories accounted for another 800,000 and nursing yet another 100,000. Many women even joined the armed forces as Wrens (Women's Royal Naval Service) or Waacs (Women's Army Auxiliary Corps), although they were not actually sent to front-line trenches. It was a tremendous response. But the greatest contribution by women was in the munitions industry, making shells and bullets. By July 1917 about 819,000 women were working in this very dangerous occupation.

About 60 per cent of all workers making shells were women. They worked 12-hour shifts, seven days a week, packing explosives and cordite into bullets and shells. Sometimes there were explosions and women were killed. Sometimes they developed lead poisoning, or diseases from the chemicals which caused their hair to fall out and turned their skins yellow (munitions girls were sometimes nicknamed 'canaries'). In general, however, they were well looked after, with women welfare supervisors, separate toilets in factories, nutritious food in

Women working alongside men in a shell-filling factory. By the end of the war as many as a million shells could be used up in less than a week

A woman shovelling coke for the Glasgow Corporation gasworks

the canteens and in many places government-provided nurseries. The pay and overtime were also good—in fact many women were actually better off during the war than they had been before it.

As a result, women also gained much greater freedom. With fewer men around, chaperones for wealthier girls became less common. Good wage-packets gave women more money to spend. They now smoked, went to the cinema, or on bicycle trips, or shopping in town, all unsupervised. Older people were scandalised, and troops returning home from France were amazed.

Their vital role in the war also gained women the vote. No one could say that they had not earned it. In June 1918 a new law gave the vote to all men over twenty-one and all women over thirty (in 1928 this was lowered to twenty-one, the same as for men). There were few complaints. The Suffragettes had won their battle by contributing to the war, not by their violent prewar methods.

Conscription and Conchies

By late 1915 it was clear to the government that even the large number of volunteers joining the Army was not going to be enough. The war was spreading to other fighting areas beyond

France and more men were needed. Machine-guns were slaughtering thousands every day. A more drastic way of recruiting men was needed, and so for the first time in British history, conscription began.

Conscription was the compulsory enlisting of men into the forces, even if they did not want to go. Certain men were exempt, particularly those with vital industrial skills, but most men between the ages of eighteen and forty-one were liable to be 'called up'. Unlike volunteers they could not choose which regiment to serve in. They were simply sent wherever they were most needed.

The Military Service Act, passed in January 1916, applied to single men only, but by May married men were included as well. As soon as young men reached the age of eighteen they could expect to be called up.

Some men totally refused to be conscripted. They were called 'conscientious objectors' because they said their consciences would not allow them to fight. People soon nicknamed them 'conchies'. Some refused for religious reasons, quoting the Bible: 'Thou shalt not kill.' Others held strong political views and thought it wrong to shoot at their working-class brothers. Whatever their reasons, however, other people called them shirkers and cowards, and they had a miserable time for the rest of the war.

Anyone who refused the call-up had to face a special court called a Military Tribunal. Some managed to convince the courts of their beliefs. In particular there were the pacifists—people who believed that killing was wrong. Some of these were willing to perform other kinds of army service. They were given ambulance work or drivers' duties. Many were sent to the front as stretcher bearers, where they faced the same risks as all the other troops, and sometimes worse as they carried wounded men back

Stretcher-bearers at Passchendaele

No.

(If replying, please quote above No.)

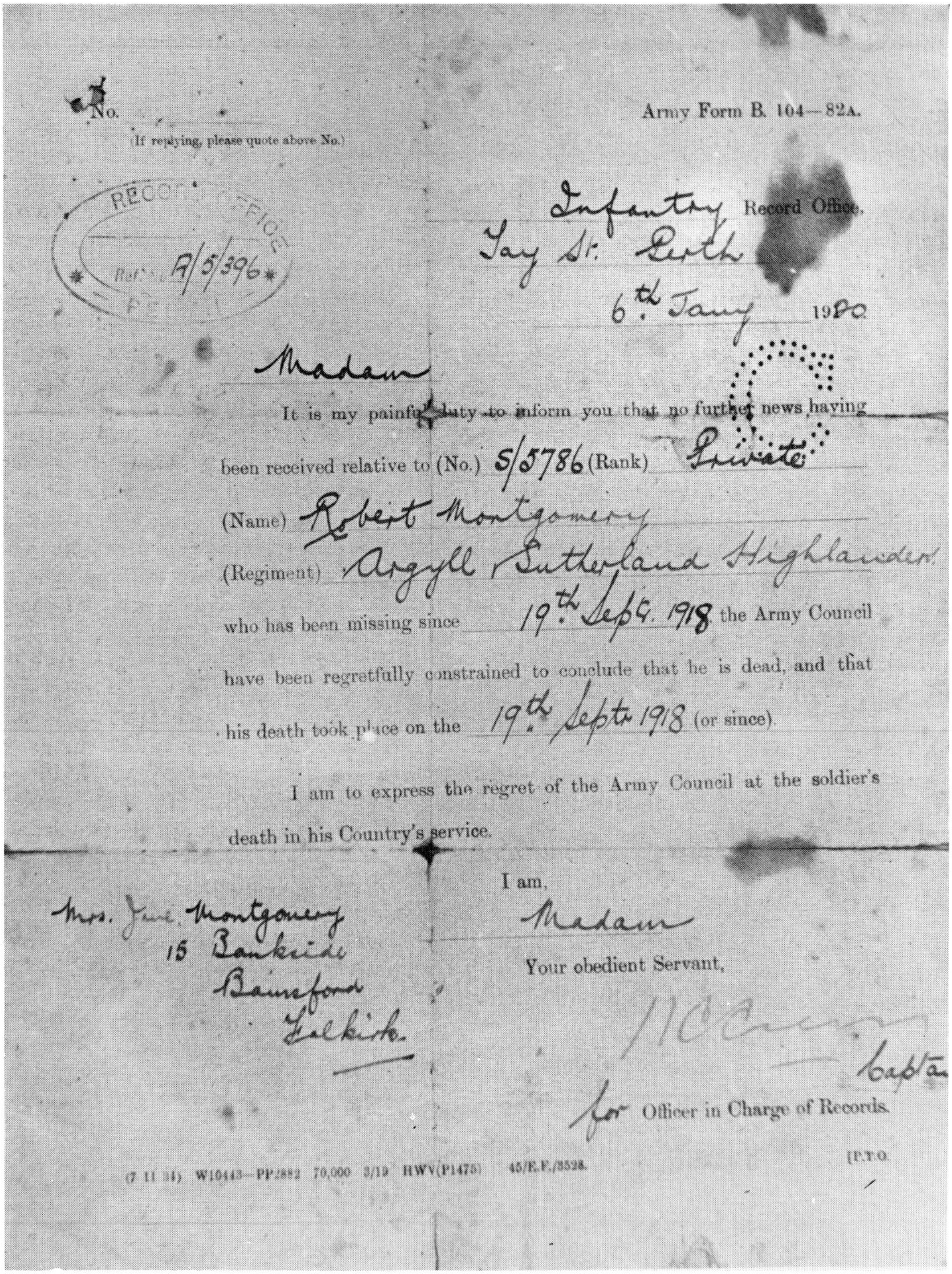

Army Form B. 104—82A.

RECORD OFFICE
Ref. No. A/5/396
PERTH

Infantry Record Office,
Tay St. Perth
6th Jany 1920

Madam

It is my painful duty to inform you that no further news having been received relative to (No.) 5/5786 (Rank) Private
(Name) Robert Montgomery
(Regiment) Argyll & Sutherland Highlanders
who has been missing since 19th Sept. 1918 the Army Council have been regretfully constrained to conclude that he is dead, and that his death took place on the 19th Sept. 1918 (or since).

I am to express the regret of the Army Council at the soldier's death in his Country's service.

I am,
Madam
Your obedient Servant,

Captain
for Officer in Charge of Records.

Mrs. Jane Montgomery
15 Bankside
Bainsford
Falkirk.

(7 11 34) W10443—PP2882 70,000 3/19 HWV(P1475) 45/E.F./3528.

[P.T.O.

The dreaded official letter. This one confirms the death of an ordinary soldier only seven weeks from the end of the war, but it was not written until January 1920. Many families did not know what had happened to their relative for months

from No-Man's-Land. Some conscientious objectors refused to do any form of military work, however, arguing that even if they did not have a gun, they would still be contributing to a war which was killing people. These men were known as 'absolutists' and were shown no sympathy by the Military Tribunals. Almost all of them were sent to prison (where they sometimes worked as farm labourers) or labour camps. Of the 6,261 who were sentenced in this way, 71 died from the harsh treatment they got and another 31 went mad.

Life in a labour camp was dreadful. The inmates were beaten, kept in solitary confinement in filthy cells, and given uncooked food. Sometimes the punishments were even worse. Men were suspended by the wrists from a rope so that their feet dangled above the ground. Others were put into wooden cages like animals. Some were thrown naked into sewage ponds or kept in pits in the ground. In protest, some men went on hunger strikes but they never won any public sympathy. Even when the war was over they stood no chance of a job; workmates, girlfriends, people in the same street, and even their families jeered at them and despised them. Strangely enough many soldiers in the trenches, also sick of the slaughter, admired the 'conchies' for having the courage to stick to their beliefs.

The British people in mourning

By the end of the war there was hardly a family in Britain not in mourning for the loss of a relative. You could tell a household in mourning by the lowered window blinds and the black clothes which the family wore every Sunday for a year.

Some families had lost relatives in Britain itself. German naval bombardments (see page 78) and air raids (see page 90) brought death and destruction into British homes. In all, about 1,500 people were killed and about 5,000 were injured in Britain. Most families, however, mourned soldiers killed in battle overseas.

News of deaths trickled back to the civilian population in many ways. Letters from wounded men mentioned friends killed. Nurses passed on news of deaths in hospitals. Army chaplains wrote to relatives of men whom they buried. Commanding officers sometimes had time to send a note to the families of men killed. Sometimes lists appeared in local papers or in shop windows giving the names of local men killed in action. And eventually the Army would send a telegram confirming what many families had already heard, but had hoped might not be true.

To begin with there was great sympathy for families who lost relatives in the war, but the Battle of the Somme changed that. This was the first mass slaughter of British troops and after that there were so many people in mourning that few bothered even to offer words of sympathy any more. Today every town and village in Britain has a war memorial where the names of local men who died in World War One are listed. There is usually another list of men killed in World War Two, but it is always shorter. For most families, World War One was much worse.

12 The End of the War

The beginning of 1917 was a vital time for both sides in the war. During 1916 the Germans had inflicted heavy losses on Russia but had failed to destroy the French at Verdun or the British Navy at Jutland. On the other hand the Allies had failed at Gallipoli and the Somme, Italy was doing badly against Austria, and Russia was on the edge of total defeat. Both sides badly needed a victory to keep their hopes alive.

The Russian Revolution

By 1917 the Russian armies were in low spirits following the failure of General Brusilov's offensive in 1916 (see Chapter 8). The Tsar Nicholas now took personal command of the troops, but he was no soldier and had no idea of war tactics. The troops continued to be pushed back deeper into Russia with heavy losses.

Russian troops deserting from the Eastern Front in 1917. One man tries to stop two others who have already thrown away their guns

Russia and the Eastern Front, 1916–1917

In addition the winter of 1916–17 was even colder than usual. Food was scarce in cities and frozen railways prevented supplies from moving. Families everywhere mourned the loss of their menfolk and anger was rising. In Petrograd, the capital (now called Leningrad), some people blamed the Tsar for Russia's failures, for he had chosen the government himself without asking the people. Now while he led the troops, his German-born wife, the Tsarina, was running the government—was its inefficiency her fault, they asked?

105

Bolshevik revolutionaries pose for a photograph beside an armoured car in Moscow, November 1917

Finally in March 1917 revolution broke out in Petrograd. Factory workers, country peasants, even soldiers and sailors in the city joined in riots. The Tsar abdicated (gave up his throne) and a new Provisional Government was formed under Alexander Kerensky. He promised to improve the running of the war, and to the country people he promised food and land. But soon it was obvious that he was unable to keep these promises. The armies continued to be driven back, and the Russian people continued to starve.

Germany now saw a chance to defeat Russia 'from the inside'. A Russian revolutionary called Lenin was secretly sent by train from Switzerland into Russia by the Germans. He was the leader of a small political party, the Bolsheviks (later called Communists). Lenin wanted power for working-class people all over the world. He thought it wrong that 'brothers' were fighting one another. And as a Russian he wanted to end the slaughter and starvation of his people. Only his party, the Bolsheviks, could do this, he believed. Kerensky's Provisional Government, which wanted to continue the war against Germany, would have to be overthrown.

Soon Lenin was calling for strikes and stirring up the people's discontent. Workers were organised into *soviets* or councils. In the trenches agitators urged troops to stop fighting and go home. For a time the soldiers did not listen, but then in the countryside many peasants overthrew their landlords and started seizing land for themselves. When this news reached the trenches many soldiers immediately deserted to join their families. Thousands of troops, sick of the slaughter and the lack of equipment, tired of always losing and fighting with old weapons, simply threw away their guns and abandoned the front lines. Whole regiments marched away. Reinforcements turned back as they heard the news. Officers stood helpless as the men just walked away from the war.

Meanwhile in Petrograd strikes and riots against Kerensky and the Provisional Government increased daily. Many placards read 'Peace! Bread! Land!'—the Bolshevik slogan. Lenin knew that most people simply wanted an end to the war, and enough to eat. Finally in November 1917 crowds attacked the Winter Palace in Petrograd, the Provisional Government's headquarters. The ministers were thrown out and a new government was formed under Lenin. One of his first acts was to make peace with Germany. By now the German Army had driven deep into Russia, but Lenin knew that one day he would win this land back again. Meanwhile he accepted its loss as the price of peace. Huge areas of fine farmland and important industrial raw materials were surrendered as Lenin signed the Treaty of Brest Litovsk with the Germans. For Russia the war with Germany was over, although years of bitter civil war lay ahead.

For the Allies, the news of Russia's surrender was a heavy blow. Now Germany could transfer all her troops to the Western Front for an attack in France.

America joins the war

The collapse of Russia late in 1917 was a serious problem for the Allies, but it would have been much worse had America not already joined the war. Why did the United States join the Allies in 1917?

At the beginning of the war, America wanted to be a neutral country. People originally from Britain and Germany had formed the two largest groups of settlers in the USA, and the government did not want a European war to stir up trouble among rival groups of supporters. The best policy was to keep out of this war altogether.

However, German submarine attacks on American shipping soon caused an outcry in the United States. On 1 May 1915 the oil tanker *Gulflight* was attacked, and only six days later the *Lusitania* was torpedoed and 128 Americans were drowned (page 83). Feelings among most Americans now ran very high and after this, 'German-Americans' had to decide where their loyalties really lay. The sinking of the *Lusitania* was an important reason for the USA's entry into the war two years later.

In January 1917 British naval intelligence intercepted a telegram from the German Foreign Secretary, Arthur Zimmermann, to the German minister in Mexico. It urged Mexico to join Germany in an alliance, and promised the Mexicans part of the state of Texas as a reward. When news of this reached the American public there was a storm of anti-German anger. America was moving closer to war.

American troops arrive in Paris in 1917. They soon won admiration for their great courage

(left to right) *Field Marshal von Hindenburg, Kaiser Wilhelm II and General Ludendorff plan the great offensive of March 1918*

Soon after this the German campaign of unrestricted U-boat warfare led to the sinking of six more American ships. This was the last straw. President Woodrow Wilson, who had actually won the 1916 election on the slogan 'He kept us out of the war', finally declared war on the Central Powers on 6 April 1917. An American Expeditionary Force was now organised under General Pershing. This was good news for the Allies. America's fresh troops and huge industrial strength would give heart to the exhausted British and French armies.

Ludendorff's great offensive, 1918

By the end of 1917 Russia had surrendered and signed the Treaty of Brest Litovsk. But several other nations, such as Greece, Portugal, Brazil and, as we have just seen, America, had joined the Allied side. Each month, more American troops were completing their training, while weapons, ships and aircraft were being mass-produced ready for the American entry into Europe.

The German army commanders now had one chance of victory. The collapse of Russia meant that they could transfer about one million troops from the Eastern Front to France.

For a time the Germans would outnumber the weary Allied troops there. The French had just mutinied (page 52) after the failure of the Nivelle Offensive, and the British had been suffering heavy losses at Passchendaele (page 54). On the other hand the British naval block-ade of Germany was now beginning to cause serious hunger among the civilian population. Germany's allies, Turkey and Austria, were both in trouble and were talking of surrender. So the Germans had to strike before the Americans arrived while they still outnumbered the Allies.

The offensive was planned and led by General Ludendorff, the hero of victories against the Russians in 1914. Because he knew that an ordinary frontal assault would fail against machine-guns, lightly equipped German 'storm troops' were trained to attack not in waves, but in small groups. In addition Ludendorff decided to attack along the whole of the front line, so that the Allies would not be able to mass in one place to hold him back. Then when he found a weak spot he would push right through.

The attack began on 21 March 1918 at 4 am. Everywhere along the front line high explosive shells pulverised the Allied defenders. Gas and

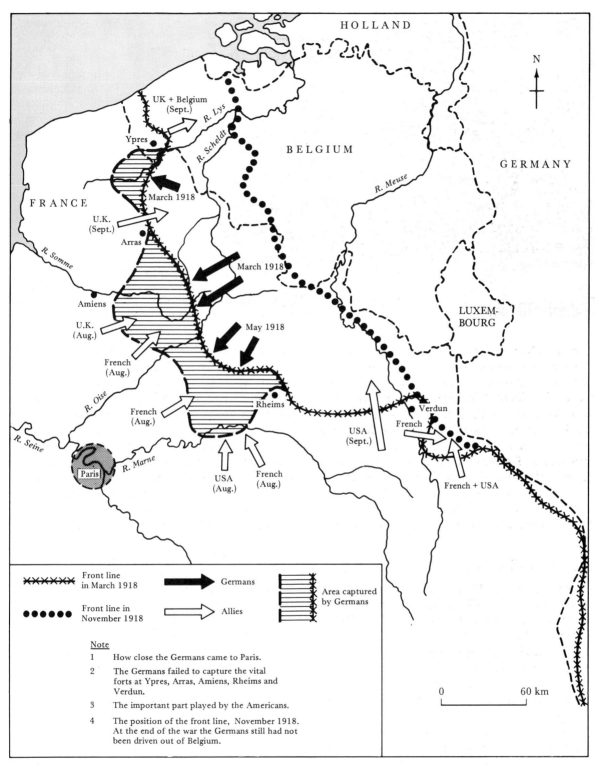

HOLLAND

UK + Belgium
(Sept.)

R. Lys

R. Scheldt

BELGIUM

GERMANY

Ypres

R. Meuse

FRANCE

March 1918

U.K.
(Sept.)

R. Somme

Arras

March 1918

LUXEM-
BOURG

Amiens

U.K.
(Aug.)

May 1918

French
(Aug.)

R. Oise

French
(Aug.)

Rheims

Verdun

USA
(Sept.)

French

R. Seine

Paris

R. Marne

USA
(Aug.)

French
(Aug.)

French + USA

N

| ✕✕✕✕✕✕ | Front line in March 1918 | ⬛➡ | Germans | | Area captured by Germans |
| ●●●●●● | Front line in November 1918 | ⬜➡ | Allies | | |

Note

1   How close the Germans came to Paris.

2   The Germans failed to capture the vital forts at Ypres, Arras, Amiens, Rheims and Verdun.

3   The important part played by the Americans.

4   The position of the front line, November 1918. At the end of the war the Germans still had not been driven out of Belgium.

0   60 km

Ludendorff's offensive and the German retreat, 1918

smoke shells followed, and then through the swirling mists came the Germans in their small assault groups. In many places visibility was less than 10 metres and the Allied troops were quickly overpowered. There was confusion everywhere and soon distress rockets were soaring into the sky from desperate defenders, cut off from help as the Germans pushed deeper into the gaps they had made.

The Germans broke through in many places. Part of their attack fell upon poorly defended trenches where they outnumbered the defenders by five to one. Soon the Allies were in retreat and it was 1914 all over again as the Germans raced for Paris. Despite the confusion, however, the Allied forces were not destroyed. A new defence line was hastily formed and troops were rushed from Italy and the Middle East to help stem the German advance. Even so the Germans pushed forward for up to 64 kilometres in some places and Paris now came within range of long-range artillery fire.

Despite their apparent success, the Germans were now exhausted and hungry. Paris, Ypres, Arras, Verdun and other cities were still in Allied hands. German spirits began to drop. They had been told the Allies were hungry and discontented but they found huge supplies of food in captured trenches. They had been told they would break through, but by July they still had not done so. In May the first Americans went into battle, and now every week brought fresh boatlands of fit, keen 'doughboys' from the USA. Worst of all, the Germans were suffering appalling casualties in this last gamble for victory. By August at least 400,000 men had been killed, wounded or captured, and this rose steadily to a final total of nearly 800,000.

The Allies hit back

On 8 August the Allies hit back against the Germans. General Ludendorff called it the 'black day of the German Army'. Canadians, Australians, Americans, Belgians, French and British troops combined to burst through the German defences and force the Germans back. At Amiens an attack by 456 tanks in a thick fog captured about 30,000 Germans and 400 field guns. It was the same all along the line. General Ludendorff later wrote:

> . . . whole bodies of our men had surrendered to single troopers, or isolated squadrons. Retiring troops meeting a fresh division going bravely into action had shouted things like 'Black-leg' and 'You're prolonging the war' . . . The officers in many places had lost their influence and allowed themselves to be swept along with the rest.

About 400,000 Germans were taken prisoner. Over 7,000 heavy guns were also captured. With losses like this the Germans could not possibly fight on and what remained of Ludendorff's army was driven back steadily. By late October the coast of Belgium had been liberated. In a single day the Allies advanced 13 kilometres from Ypres, which was more than they had managed in months of bitter fighting the year before.

The collapse of Germany

Although the German Army was still fighting in France and Belgium, events elsewhere finally brought the war to an end. From the beginning of the war the British Navy had blockaded German seaports, and soon the effects of this began to be felt. Industry ran short of fuel and chemicals for explosives and gas. In 1915 rationing began in Germany. In 1916 food riots broke out in many German cities as people demanded bread—the winter of 1917 was called the 'turnip winter'. By 1918 starvation had hit millions of Germans: it has been calculated that about 120,000 people died from hunger in 1916. This rose to 260,000 in 1917 and to 290,000 in 1918. Most of these people were either very young or very old. Those who survived queued for whatever food they could get, as a wave of discontent swept through Germany. Better to surrender and live, than fight on and die of starvation, many said. By 1918 there were strikes and riots as the civilian population demanded an end to the war.

Meanwhile Germany's allies were also collapsing. Driven back by Serbian and French

King George V (centre, with beard) *meets French children in a village near Ypres on 2 December 1918, three weeks after Armistice Day*

troops during 1918, the Bulgarian Army surrendered on 29 September. A month later on 30 October the Turkish forces also surrendered, as Lawrence's Arabs and General Allenby's army reached Damascus and British troops in Mesopotamia pressed on past Baghdad (page 74). On 3 November the forces of the Austro-Hungarian Empire surrendered as Czech, Polish and other troops mutinied against the hated Austrians. Germany was left to fight on alone.

At the same time mutinies broke out in Germany. On 29 October the sailors at Kiel naval base went on strike. Although 600 were arrested this did not stop the trouble. On 4 November they mutinied again and 100,000 seamen seized control of their ships, demanding an end to the war. More naval mutinies broke out in other harbours, and there were army riots in several cities. The war-weary troops had had enough.

A flu epidemic already spreading across Europe now hit the German population. Thousands died, especially those already weak from hunger.

On 9 November there was a general strike in the German capital, Berlin. Crowds marched through the streets demanding an end to the war. The government resigned and the Kaiser fled to Holland where he lived in exile until his death in 1941.

It was impossible to fight on. German civilians were starving. German industry had no fuel or chemicals. Strikes and riots were spreading to dozens of German cities. Germany's allies had all surrendered and the German Army, though still in France and Belgium, was being driven steadily back.

The armistice

On 9 November the new German government asked the Allies for an armistice (or cease-fire). The Allies made certain demands: the

111

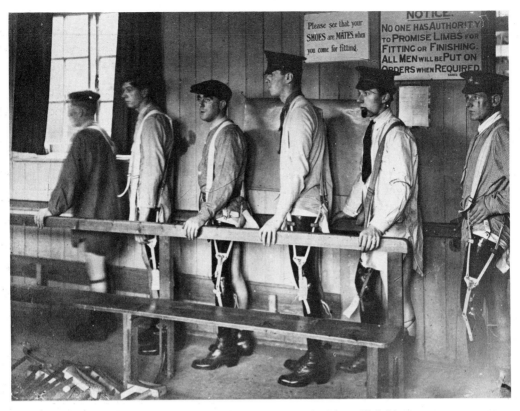

The cost of war. Soldiers being fitted with artificial legs

Germans had to withdraw from the rest of Belgium and France, surrender all weapons and release all prisoners-of-war, surrender all U-boats and warships, and allow Allied troops into Germany. The Germans agreed and the ceasefire began at 11 o'clock on the morning of 11 November, 1918.

As the clocks struck eleven in London, crowds poured onto the streets to celebrate. A din of car horns, bicycle bells, trumpets, church bells, police whistles, dustbin lids and (especially) cheering people rang through the city to mark the end of the war.

In the trenches the soldiers also celebrated. At ten to eleven an officer led his men in a charge on a bridge—they were all killed by machine-guns. But as eleven o'clock came the last of the firing died away along the front lines. There was a pause. Then cautiously the troops shouted to one another and hesitantly showed their heads above the parapets. In some places

they sang songs of relief and joy. Soon they met to exchange sweets and cigarettes, or to share a bottle of wine. Mostly they were just thankful to have survived. At last they would be able to leave their filthy dug-outs.

That night rockets and flares rose into the sky like a firework display. For many, however, the memories of terrible sights and appalling slaughter would never fade.

Why did Germany lose the war?

1 The Schlieffen Plan failed at the very start, forcing the Germans to fight in two directions at once.
2 Germany's allies were not as effective as she was, even though the Turks won at Gallipoli.
3 Except for U-boats, the Germans had no control of the sea. The High Seas fleet hardly went to sea at all after Jutland in 1916.
4 The German U-boats did not force Britain

into surrender. Convoys and other measures defeated the U-boat threat.

5 Britain's control of the sea allowed her to blockade Germany so completely that vital food and industrial supplies were cut off. This caused a shortage of essential war materials and produced widespread starvation which caused Germany to collapse.

6 Germany's U-boat campaign, and the Zimmermann telegram, brought the USA into the war. American strength in men and industry gave a huge advantage to the Allied side.

7 Germany's last great attack in 1918 failed. Any last chance of victory therefore disappeared.

The human cost of the war

Before the war no one realised how many people would be killed. No one realised either how many civilians would be affected.

At least 100,000 civilians died—in torpedoed ships, in air raids, or murdered by troops. In addition, about 4 million Armenians and Jews were massacred by Turkey. Starvation killed many more: at least 2 million in Russia, 1 million in Serbia and Austria, 800,000 in Germany, another 800,000 in Romania, and 30,000 in Belgium.

Soldiers killed fighting for the British Empire included:

Great Britain	761,000
India	62,000
Australia	59,000
Canada	57,000
New Zealand	16,000
South Africa	7,000
Newfoundland	1,000

About 10 million soldiers were killed in the First World War. About 20 million soldiers were shot, gassed, blinded, shell-shocked, burned or maimed. Five men died every minute of the war.

No one really knows exactly how many soldiers died, but here is a rough estimate of each country's losses:

	killed	*wounded*
Germany	1,900,000	4,250,000
Russia	1,700,000	4,950,000
France	1,400,000	2,500,000
Austria-Hungary	1,300,000	3,620,000
Britain and Empire	998,000	2,300,000
Italy	615,000	947,000
Turkey	350,000	450,000
Romania	340,000	510,000
USA	116,000	205,000
Bulgaria	95,000	155,000
Serbia	50,000	134,000
Belgium	44,000	45,000
Portugal	7,500	14,000
Greece	5,500	9,000
Montenegro	3,500	6,000
Japan	400	1,200

13 The Treaty of Versailles

The German Army surrendered on 11 November 1918. It was time for the victorious Allies to make a peace treaty with Germany. Thirty-two Allied nations met for the Peace Conference at the Palace of Versailles, near Paris. Here they discussed how best to deal with Germany, now that the fighting was over.

The 'Big Four'

Representatives attended from all the Allied countries except Russia, but the conference was actually dominated by a few top politicians. They were President Clemenceau of France, Prime Minister Lloyd George of Britain, President Woodrow Wilson from the United States, and President Orlando of Italy. They represented the most powerful nations on the Allied side and were soon nicknamed the 'Big Four' (although Italy was less important than the others because the Italians had won so few battles in the war). Unfortunately, the four men had different ideas on how Germany should be dealt with.

Clemenceau bitterly hated the Germans. His country had suffered the most casualties, and the most damage to roads, railways, industries, towns and farming. He wanted revenge, and demanded that the punishment for Germany should be as severe as possible. The Germans should be forced to pay for all the damage and deaths they had caused. Germany should also be made so weak that she could never attack France again.

Some delegates protested that Clemenceau was being too harsh, but he was determined. He pointed out that the Germans forced a very harsh peace treaty on the defeated Russians at Brest Litovsk (page 107) and would probably have done the same to the Allies, had Britain and France lost. Moreover the Germans had started the war, by their actions before 1914 and by encouraging Austria to attack Serbia in July 1914, so it was quite reasonable to punish them severely now. As Chairman of the Peace Conference, he was able to press his views strongly—so strongly that he earned the nickname 'Tiger' Clemenceau.

America's President Wilson took the opposite view. He believed that the best answer was to let the Germans off lightly. He urged everyone to lay weapons and hatred aside and concentrate on making a new, peaceful Europe for the future. He argued that if the Germans were punished harshly, they would feel resentful, and would one day want revenge. This would only lead to another war. America had not suffered very badly from the war, and this forgiving attitude was more understandable.

Lloyd George stood somewhere in the middle. He could see that the Germans would feel bitter if they were forced to sign a harsh treaty, but the British public wanted revenge. Slogans like 'Hang the Kaiser' and 'Squeeze Germany till the pips squeak' were popular. Lloyd George had won the General Election of 1918 by promising the people revenge on Germany at Versailles, and in the end he moved towards Clemenceau's viewpoint.

Orlando was less important. The Italians had joined the war in 1915 after being promised additional land in the Mediterranean area (page 74). Versailles was the chance to gain an empire at the expense of Austria and Turkey. However, the Italians had done little to help win the war and most delegates at the conference were not very interested as Orlando demanded more land for Italy.

President Wilson's Fourteen Points

President Wilson was anxious to create a new, peaceful Europe. As a step towards this he produced fourteen suggestions which he said would help avoid future wars. These were his Fourteen Points:

1 There should be no secret diplomacy or groups of alliances like the Triple Entente or Triple Alliance. (Knowing you had allies encouraged you to make war.)

2 Neutral ships should be allowed to sail anywhere without being stopped by ships from any other country. (Both Britain and Germany had stopped and searched neutral ships during the war.)

3 Restrictions preventing trade between certain nations should be abolished. (This would ease trade rivalries.)

4 Every country should greatly reduce the size of its army and navy.

5 The Allies should not share out the German colonies amongst themselves. (This would be taking unfair advantage of Germany's defeat.)

6 Russia should be left alone to develop her own system of government. (Many nations disapproved of communism, but Wilson could see that interfering in Russian would only cause more trouble.)

7 All German troops should leave Belgium.

8 Alsace and Lorraine should be returned to France.

9 The Austrian-Italian border should be redrawn so that people could live in the country of their choice. (Many people who spoke Italian lived over the frontier in Austria and wanted to be part of Italy.)

10 The minority peoples of the Austro-Hungarian Empire should be given independence. (Bosnians, Czechs, Romanians and many others had hated their Austrian rulers and wanted freedom, so Wilson suggested creating new countries for them.)

11 The people in the Balkans should also be free to rule themselves.

12 Arab people in the Turkish Empire should be given independence and the Dardanelles should be open to ships from all countries.

13 Poland, which had been swallowed up by Germany, Russia and Austria in 1795, should be re-created. (The Poles did not want to be governed by foreigners.)

14 A 'League of Nations' should be formed, in which countries could negotiate instead of fighting, so that quarrels and rivalries could be settled without war.

Many of Wilson's points were attempts to give freedom to discontented peoples, by creating new countries in which they could rule themselves. Most of his other suggestions were also aimed at preventing future wars. However, President Clemenceau of France was so determined to crush the Germans, at the same time leaving his own country in a very powerful position, that some of Wilson's points were ignored.

The terms of the Treaty of Versailles

Eventually, after much argument, the Allies produced their treaty. President Wilson's idea of making states for the various minority peoples was accepted, and several new countries were created by the politicians at Versailles.

They decided to create nation-states, or a country for each people. They also decided that each of these new countries would have to be able to fend for itself, so frontiers were specially drawn to include coalfields, good farmland, and easily defended borders.

In addition, because the French were determined that the Germans should not be able to attack them again, the German armed forces were drastically cut in size. The Germans were also forced to pay for all war damage, and to accept total responsibility for starting the war. These were the main effects of the Treaty of Versailles:

1 *Germany lost a lot of land* (compare the two maps of Europe on the next page)

(a) Alsace and Lorraine were returned to France.

(b) Part of eastern Germany was taken away to help make the country of Poland. Land which Germany had won from Russia in 1917 was also used to make Poland

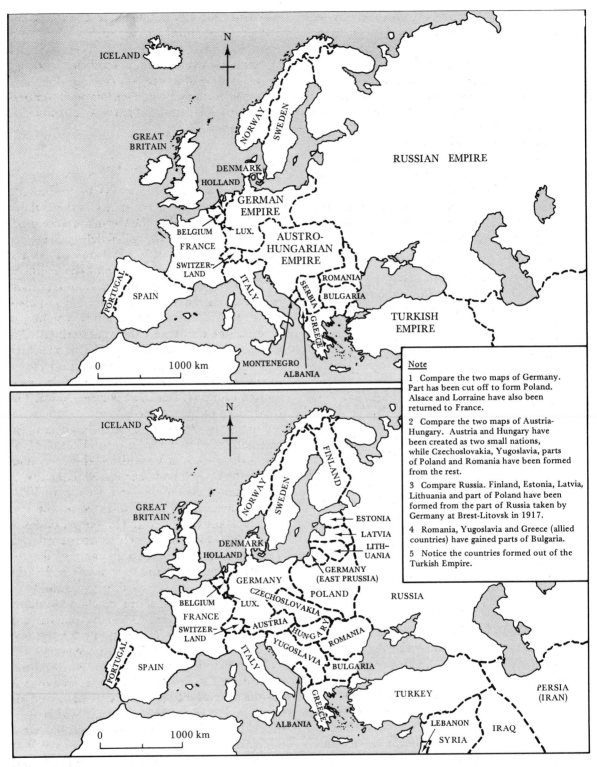

Note

1 Compare the two maps of Germany. Part has been cut off to form Poland. Alsace and Lorraine have also been returned to France.

2 Compare the two maps of Austria-Hungary. Austria and Hungary have been created as two small nations, while Czechoslovakia, Yugoslavia, parts of Poland and Romania have been formed from the rest.

3 Compare Russia. Finland, Estonia, Latvia, Lithuania and part of Poland have been formed from the part of Russia taken by Germany at Brest-Litovsk in 1917.

4 Romania, Yugoslavia and Greece (allied countries) have gained parts of Bulgaria.

5 Notice the countries formed out of the Turkish Empire.

Europe before and after the Treaty of Versailles

(remember that Russia and Germany had swallowed up Poland a hundred years earlier). As a result, part of Germany, East Prussia, was separated from the rest of Germany by part of Poland.

(c) The Silesian Coalfield, in eastern Germany, was given to Poland to give the new country some industry.

(d) The Saar Coalfield, in western Germany, was given to France for fifteen years as compensation for the destruction of French coalfields in the war.

(e) All Germany's overseas colonies were taken away and put under the control of various Allied countries.

2 Germany was stripped of her military power

(a) The German Army was reduced to a mere 100,000 men (it had been about 4 million 1914). This was smaller even than the Belgian Army.

(b) Germany was not allowed to have any troops or military defences in the Rhineland—the area between the River Rhine and the French border. This would make it difficult for Germany ever to attack France or Belgium again.

(c) The entire German Navy was handed over to the Allies (although the Germans deliberately sank all their ships after handing them over at Scapa Flow). Germany was allowed to keep six smaller battleships, but was especially forbidden submarines.

(d) The entire German Air Force was handed over to the Allies and Germany was forbidden to have any war planes at all.

(e) The German Army was forbidden to have tanks.

3 Germany was made to pay for the war

Germany was forced to pay compensation for the deaths and damage caused by the war. This included pensions for all war widows and war wounded, and compensation for the loss of French and Belgian farm and industrial production. It also included compensation for the destruction of all roads, railways, houses, schools and so on. A committee of Allied businessmen estimated that this should come to the enormous total of £6,000 million.

Germany, already exhausted by the war, could not possibly afford to pay such a huge sum, even in annual instalments. As a result French troops took over German coalfields and factories and confiscated everything they produced as part payment. This financial compensation for lives and property was known as 'reparations'.

Reaction to the Treaty

Sometimes a defeated nation is allowed to take part in making the peace treaty at the end of a war, but at Versailles the Germans were made to sit and wait while the Allied delegates argued about the terms. President Wilson was sick and could not press his more peaceful viewpoint. So 'Tiger' Clemenceau got his way and Germany was crushed. The Germans had no say at all in the future of their country. They just had to listen as the terms were dictated to them. One German general said sadly, 'The hand which signs this, signs its own death warrant', for it meant agreeing to the destruction of the great German Empire. But there was no choice. The treaty had to be accepted.

Finally, on 28 June 1919, the German representatives were called into the Hall of Mirrors at the Palace of Versailles—the very room where the French had been forced to sign away Alsace and Lorraine to the Germans in 1871. Two thousand delegates watched as the two sad Germans were escorted in like prisoners. A silence fell while they meekly signed as ordered. Then conversation started up again while outside cannons roared and crowds cheered as the two pale Germans were led away again.

When news of the terms reached Germany there was an outcry. Germans particularly resented having the entire blame for the war put on them—they felt they had been provoked by Britain and France. Later, when Hitler overturned the Treaty of Versailles by expanding the army, building up a huge navy and air force, and taking back the lands which Germany had lost in 1919, many people were happy to follow him.

Even among the Allies some people felt that the treaty was too harsh. President Wilson cer-

*A poster warns Belgian children to keep away from unexploded shells (1919).
People are still being killed or maimed today by First World War bombs*

tainly thought so, and even Lloyd George said in the House of Commons, '. . . they are terrible terms . . . There is no doubt that they are stern. Are they just?' The French army commander Marshal Foch described the terms as only 'a twenty-year ceasefire'; and twenty years later the Second World War began.

Austria and Turkey after the war

The Treaty of Versailles dealt only with Germany. Separate treaties were made with all the other countries which had fought on the German side. Under the terms of the Treaty of Saint-Germain, which dealt with Austria, the old Austro-Hungarian Empire was broken up and the minority peoples now got their chance to have their own separate states. The Serbs, Bosnians and other Slav peoples of the south-ern part of the old empire were given a new country called Yugoslavia. In the north, a small part of the old empire was added to the new Poland, while the rest was formed into the country of Czechoslovakia. To the east, another part was confiscated and given to Romania (an allied country). Austria and Hungary were left as two small countries without any empire at all.

As a result of the Treaty of Lausanne the Turkish Empire was also broken up. New countries were created for the various Arab tribes which had helped Britain during the war. These included Lebanon, Syria, Iraq, Jordan and Saudi Arabia. Turkey was left a much smaller country, also without an empire.

Finally, Bulgaria, a German ally, lost land to Greece, which was a British ally. Finland and the small countries of Latvia, Estonia and

Lithuania were all created out of territories lost by Russia to Germany in 1917 (see the map of Europe).

Europe after Versailles

By 1919 Europe was a completely different continent from the Europe of 1914. The old empires of Russia, Germany, Austria-Hungary and Turkey had disappeared. New, smaller countries now replaced them, states specially created so that smaller groups of people could be free to govern themselves. Meanwhile Britain and France had more colonies and seemed to be more powerful than ever. In Russia the people faced the future under the world's first Communist government. The United States, having helped the Allies win the war, was now determined to leave Europe to solve its own problems.

Shattered towns, farms, businesses and industries faced a struggle towards recovery. Governments had huge debts to pay. Homeless refugees wandering around Europe had to be found countries to live in. Thousands of unexploded mines and shells had to be cleared away before they killed even more people. Thousands of prisoners of war had to be sent home. New countries like Poland and Yugoslavia had to build up trade with the rest of the world. Maimed and blinded men had to face the future as cripples and invalids. Millions of widows had to support families by themselves.

In 1914 the men of all nations had marched off to war believing that this would be the 'war to end war'. But in 1939 the Germans followed Adolf Hitler into a second world war and another generation of Europe's young men was slaughtered.

Index